Beginning Unreal Engine 4 Blueprints Visual Scripting

Using C++: From Beginner to Pro

Satheesh Pv

Apress®

Beginning Unreal Engine 4 Blueprints Visual Scripting

Satheesh Pv
Mumbai, India

ISBN-13 (pbk): 978-1-4842-6395-2   ISBN-13 (electronic): 978-1-4842-6396-9
https://doi.org/10.1007/978-1-4842-6396-9

Copyright © 2021 by Satheesh Pv

Managing Director, Apress Media LLC: Welmoed Spahr
Acquisitions Editor: Spandana Chatterjee
Development Editor: Matthew Moodie
Coordinating Editor: Divya Modi

Cover designed by eStudioCalamar

Cover image designed by Pixabay

Distributed to the book trade worldwide by Springer Science+Business Media New York, 1 New York Plaza, Suite 4600, New York, NY 10004-1562, USA. Phone 1-800-SPRINGER, fax (201) 348-4505, e-mail orders-ny@springer-sbm.com, or visit www.springeronline.com. Apress Media, LLC is a California LLC and the sole member (owner) is Springer Science + Business Media Finance Inc (SSBM Finance Inc). SSBM Finance Inc is a **Delaware** corporation.

For information on translations, please e-mail booktranslations@springernature.com; for reprint, paperback, or audio rights, please e-mail bookpermissions@springernature.com.

Apress titles may be purchased in bulk for academic, corporate, or promotional use. eBook versions and licenses are also available for most titles. For more information, reference our Print and eBook Bulk Sales web page at http://www.apress.com/bulk-sales.

Any source code or other supplementary material referenced by the author in this book is available to readers on GitHub via the book's product page, located at www.apress.com/978-1-4842-6395-2. For more detailed information, please visit http://www.apress.com/source-code.

Printed on acid-free paper

*Thanks to Jesus for His guidance and to
my wife, mother, and brother for their continuous
support, and a big thanks to Apress for giving me the
opportunity to write this book*

Table of Contents

About the Author

Satheesh Pv is a game programmer living in Mumbai, India. He started his career as a game developer in 2012 by making a first-person multiplayer game with his brother and close friend using the Unreal Development Kit. Satheesh created Unreal X-Editor, an IDE developed for UnrealScript, the native scripting language of Unreal Engine 3. He was selected by Epic Games as one of the closed beta-testers for Unreal Engine 4 before its public release. He is also a moderator at Unreal Engine forums and a spotlight member and engine contributor.

About the Technical Reviewer

 **Pranav Paharia** is a game developer who has worked on game technologies like Cocos2dx, Unity3D, and Unreal Engine 4. He has a bachelor's degree in information technology and a postgraduate degree in game development. After realizing his die-hard interest in games, he started his career in game development by working for Indie Game Studios making mobile games in many genres. One of the projects he worked on, *Song of Swords*, won the NASSCOM 2013 People's Choice of the Year Award. He has worked on a variety of systems for games, including gameplay, multiplayer, data pipelines, and cinematics. He is proficient in C++ and C# and can work on any game technology to create mind-boggling simulations. He is a self-taught programmer and designer.

Since 2013, Pranav has created simulations for single-player games, multiplayer games, card games, VR games, AR simulations, serious games, training simulations, and learning games. He has also worked on a few game development books. With his vast experience in creating simulations, he is now involved in solving real-life problems using the latest technologies, such as creating architectural visualizations, VR training systems, and medical data imaging for clients like DRDO India, Zaha Hadid, Line Creative, and MediaMonks.

ABOUT THE TECHNICAL REVIEWER

Apart from developing graphical simulations, Pranav is currently working on creating virtual productions tech using Unreal Engine. He is an avid gamer who loves Dota 2. He also has keen interest in photography, reading books with philosophical context, and riding his bike on long road trips. He is grateful to Krsna for guiding him through his purpose in life. You can contact him at pranavpaharia@gmail.com; also check out his website at www.pranavpaharia.com.

Introduction

This book covers the basics of Unreal Engine, including Blueprints, materials, and C++. It starts with downloading Unreal Engine using Epic Games Launcher and using the GitHub version. From there, it moves forward to Blueprint classes and the common classes, such as Game Mode, Game State, Game Instance, and Player Controller. You learn about how to add C++ and get a brief introduction to Unreal C++, materials, and physics. At the end of the book, you make a small demo game extended from a first-person template using Blueprints. In this demo game, you learn how to add ammo and ammo pickup.

This book is primarily aimed at beginners who want to learn more about the Engine, how a project is structured, Unreal Blueprints, and C++.

CHAPTER 1

Introduction to Unreal Engine 4

Hello there, and welcome to this beginner's guide to Unreal Engine 4. Throughout this book, you learn about different aspects of Unreal Engine 4, and you learn to create a sample game with the knowledge you gain. In this chapter, you learn how to download Unreal Engine through Epic Games Launcher and GitHub. After that, you learn how a project is structured and become familiar with the Unreal Editor interface.

Getting Unreal Engine

This chapter looks at how you acquire Unreal Engine. You can download it through either Epic Games Launcher or GitHub. Either way, you need to create an account at www.unrealengine.com, which is free.

First, let's look at the differences between Epic Games Launcher and GitHub.

© Satheesh Pv 2021
S. Pv, *Beginning Unreal Engine 4 Blueprints Visual Scripting*,
https://doi.org/10.1007/978-1-4842-6396-9_1

- The Epic Games Launcher version (a.k.a. the binary version or vanilla version) of Unreal Engine 4 comes with the engine prebuilt, and you can select the platforms you need. You can also select the engine source, starter template, feature packs, and so forth, if you need them. The binary version does not support creating dedicated servers for your game, so if you are planning to develop a multiplayer game with a dedicated server, you must use the source version.

- The GitHub version (a.k.a. the source version) gives you the entire source code of the engine without any binaries, so you need to compile it manually. The source code version of the engine is typically used by developers who want to fix the engine's bugs or add new features. This version is also required if your game relies on a dedicated server. The prerequisites for the source code version of the engine are Visual Studio 2019 (or higher) on Windows or Xcode on macOS.

Download from Epic Games Launcher

If you don't have an Epic Games account, you need to create one at www.unrealengine.com/id/register.

If you do have an Epic Games account, then head over to www.unrealengine.com/en-US/get-now and select your license to download and install Epic Games Launcher for your platform. After installation, open the launcher, and log in using your credentials. You should see the screenshot shown Figure 1-1.

Figure 1-1. *Epic Games Launcher with engine version4.24 installed*

Near the ENGINE VERSIONS tab, you can see a + button, which allows you to download and install any engine version you want.

Download from GitHub

If you prefer to work with the source version of the engine, you can do so by downloading the engine source code and compiling it yourself, but you must have Visual Studio 2019 (with C++ support enabled) installed if you use Windows or Xcode if you are on macOS.

First, you must create a GitHub account (it's free) and log in to your Epic Games account. Once logged in, go to your account dashboard in Epic Games and link your GitHub account. After this, you are ready to download the full source code for Unreal Engine 4.

Downloading Source Code

Once you have access to the Unreal Engine repository, you can click the **Clone or download** button and select the **Download ZIP** button (as seen in Figure 1-2).

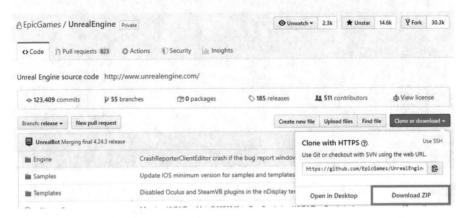

Figure 1-2. *Download ZIP button in Unreal Engine Git repository*

Cloning the Unreal Engine Repository

To clone a repository, you need to have a Git client installed. Cloning is the process of downloading or copying a repository into an empty folder in your working machine, including the full Git history, so you can use Git commands. You only download the source code without any Git files, so you won't track changes or have any information about previous commits.

I use SourceTree from Atlassian.

Note   If you prefer other tools, please visit https://git-scm.com/download/gui/windows for Windows or https://git-scm.com/download/gui/mac for macOS.

After installing SourceTree, open the application. In the new tab, select **Add an account**. In the new window, switch the hosting service to GitHub and select the **Refresh OAuth Token** button. Once SourceTree has access to your repos, you can select **Unreal Engine repo** from your repositories list and then select **Clone**. This lets you choose a path to save the files. Under **Advanced Options,** select the **release** branch and click the **Clone** button.

Once cloning is done or after downloading the ZIP file, go to the directory and double-click the **Setup.bat** file. (If you downloaded the ZIP file, extract it first). You can include or exclude specific platforms by passing the necessary flags in the Setup.bat file. For example, to exclude Mac and iOS platforms on a Windows machine, you can run Setup.bat like this:

```
Setup.bat --exclude=Mac --exclude=iOS
```

This ensures that any dependencies and files required for the Mac and iOS platforms are skipped. Once Setup.bat finishes, run **GenerateProjectFiles.bat**, which generates the UE4 solution file that you can open in Visual Studio. After opening the solution file, you can see UE4 under the Engine folder in Solution Explorer. Right-click UE4 and select Build. This starts the build process, which might take an hour or more to compile, depending on your hardware.

Getting to Know Unreal Editor

Now that you have installed (or compiled) your engine, let's start it up. Throughout this book, we only work with the binary version of the engine, which is 4.24. You create a blank project and learn about the aspects of the engine. To start the engine, click the Launch button for 4.24.3. This opens the **Unreal Project Browser** window, where you can select an existing project or create a new one from scratch or a template (see Figure 1-3).

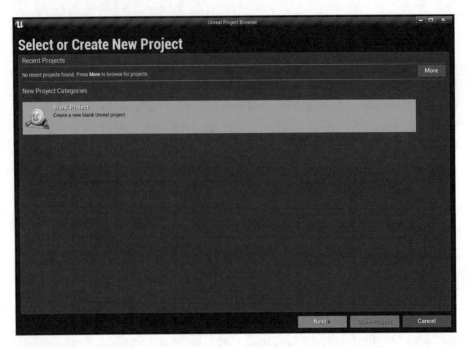

Figure 1-3.

Let's select **Blank Project** and click Next. On the next page, you are prompted to either start a blank project or create one based on a template. For our purposes, let's select a blank template and click Next. This gives you a project with no code or content and with the default settings. Finally, the last page allows you to do basic configuration and name your project.

Let's go through the Project Settings page shown in Figure 1-4.

Figure 1-4.

- **Blueprint** (labeled 1 in the screenshot) lets you choose whether your project is based on Blueprints or C++. If you start in Blueprints, you can later add C++ code to your project.

- Depending on your project, you can change **Maximum Quality** (labeled 2 in the screenshot) to **Scalable 3D/2D**. The first option is suitable for PCs/consoles, and the second option is suitable for mobile.

- If you target high-end PC games and own an Nvidia RTX graphics card, you can enable **raytracing** features (labeled 3 in the screenshot) for your game.

- **Desktop/Console** (labeled 4 in the screenshot) lets you select the closest equivalent target platform.

- **With Starter Content** (labeled 5 in the screenshot) lets you choose if you want to copy starter content to your project. It contains simple meshes with basic materials.

- **Folder** (labeled 6 in the screenshot) is where you enter the location of the project's folder.

- **Name** (labeled 7 in the screenshot) is where you enter the name of your newly created project.

To create the project, click the **Create Project** button. This starts the engine with an empty project ready for you to create.

Project Structure

Next, let's look at the project folder you just created to see how a project is structured. If you navigate to the project folder, you should see a structure similar to the screenshot shown in Figure 1-5.

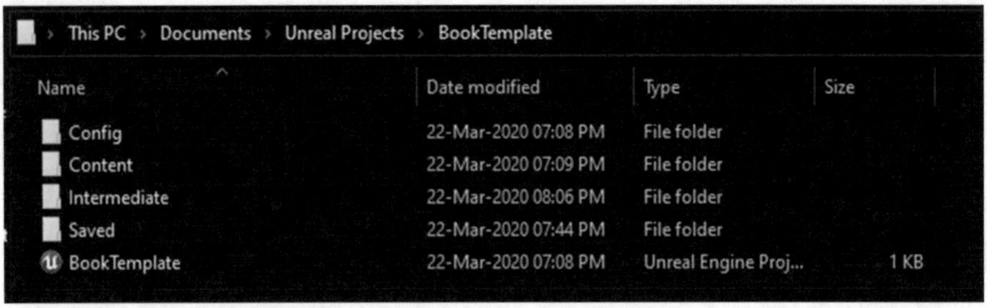

Name	Date modified	Type	Size
Config	22-Mar-2020 07:08 PM	File folder	
Content	22-Mar-2020 07:09 PM	File folder	
Intermediate	22-Mar-2020 08:06 PM	File folder	
Saved	22-Mar-2020 07:44 PM	File folder	
BookTemplate	22-Mar-2020 07:08 PM	Unreal Engine Proj...	1 KB

This PC › Documents › Unreal Projects › BookTemplate

Figure 1-5. *An example project (note that the project name might differ)*

- **Config**: This folder is where the settings are saved when you change editor preferences or project settings. You can also create your config files to save data.

- **Content**: This folder is where all your game assets are saved.

- **Intermediate**: Editor and game temporary files are generated here. It is safe to delete this folder, and it is automatically regenerated when the editor is started next.

- **Saved**: This folder contains all the autogenerated config files, log files, and autosaves.

The following are other folders that you might see.

- **Binaries**: This folder contains the DLL files for your project. It only appears if your project contains C++ source code.

- **DerivedDataCache**: This folder contains versions of your assets on its target platforms. You can safely delete this folder, and the editor regenerates it next time.

- **Source**: This folder contains header (.h) and source (.cpp) files. It only appears if your project contains C++ source code.

- **Plugins**: This folder contains all the plugins for your project. To create a new plugin, your project must contain C++.

An Unreal Editor Tour

Once the engine starts, your screen should look similar to Figure 1-6.

9

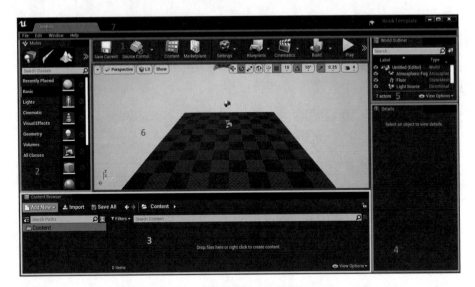

Figure 1-6. *Default Unreal Editor user interface*

Let's go through the layout of the Unreal Editor as seen in Figure 1-6.

- The area labeled 1 is the **toolbar**. Here you can save the current scene, open the Content Browser, access quick settings, build lighting, Play In Editor, and so forth.

- The area labeled 2 is the **Modes panel**. Here you can switch between different modes, such as Placing Actors mode (default), Mesh Paint mode, Landscape mode, Foliage mode, and Brush mode.

- The area labeled 3 is the **Content Browser** where you import or create all the assets.

- The area labeled 4 is the **Details panel**, where you modify the properties of the selected actor that is placed inside a level.

- The area labeled 5 is **World Outliner**. It shows all actors currently present inside the level. Using the eye icon, you can quickly hide/unhide actors.

- The area labeled the **menu bar**. It allows you to add a new C++ class, access editor and project settings, reopen closed tabs, and so forth.

The Toolbar

The toolbar is displayed right above the viewport. It provides easy access to various editor commands.

- **Save**: Saves the current scene. If the current scene is not saved, it prompts the user to select a location to save the map.

- **Source Control**: Provides access to different source controls, like Perforce, Git, Subversion, and so forth. You can install other source control plugins too. Source control is the practice of tracking and managing changes to code or assets. You can read more about source control at https://en.wikipedia.org/wiki/Version_control.

- **Content**: Opens the Content Browser.

- **Marketplace**: Opens the UE4 marketplace in your default browser.

- **Settings**: Gives quick access to some editor settings, as well as Project Settings and World Settings.

- **Blueprints**: Creates a new Blueprint class or opens a Level Blueprint. You learn more about Blueprints in the next chapter.

- **Cinematics**: Adds level or master sequences.

- **Build**: Builds lighting, navigation, geometry, and so forth. This button is disabled when Play In Session is active, or the current level is previewing in less than Shader Model 5.

- **Play**: Plays the current level in the active viewport. The arrow next to the Play button shows a drop-down with options that let the developer play the game in a new window, mobile preview, as a stand-alone game, and so forth. You can also set the game to start a dedicated server for testing multiplayer games.

- **Launch**: Launches the current level in a given device.

Modes

The Modes panel switches between various tool modes for the editor. Each mode panel can be switched by pressing **Shift + *1 to 5***.

- **Place mode (Shift+1)**: Places actors in a scene.

- **Paint mode (Shift+2)**: Allows you to vertex paint a Static Mesh Actor directly on the viewport. This means you can paint color data onto the vertices of the Static Mesh Actor that is placed on the level and use that information in the material assigned to that Static Mesh.

- **Landscape mode (Shift+3)**: Creates new landscapes or edits existing ones.

- **Foliage mode (Shift+4)**: Paints foliage.

- **Brush mode (Shift+5)**: Modifies BSP (binary space partitioning) brushes. It is a geometry tool to quickly prototype or block-out levels.

Content Browser

The Content Browser is the heart of your project. All the assets that make up your blockbuster game reside here. You can import supported file types and create new assets like Blueprint, Materials, and Sequences. The Content Browser allows you to favorite your assets and arrange them in your own collections for quick access, which improves your workflow significantly. So let's look at them.

Favorites

You can assign any folder as favorites for quick access. Favorites is not enabled by default. You can enable it by clicking View Options in the bottom-right corner of the Content Browser and selecting Show Favorites. The Favorites section is visible above the main Content folder.

Note   Only folders can be assigned as favorites, not assets.

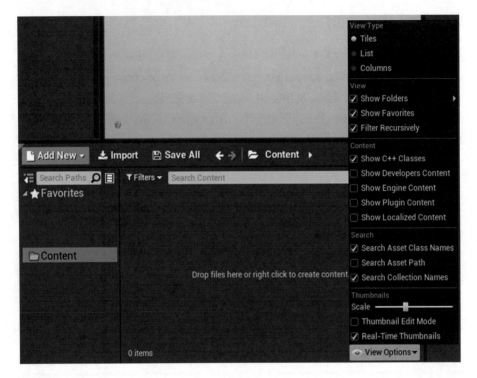

Figure 1-7.

Collections

Collections allow you to organize your assets into separate collections. For example, if you are making an open-world game, you can make different collections for player buildings, urban buildings, objective buildings, quest props, and so on. Each collection can have child collections, and assets can be added or removed anytime. Removing an item from a collection does not remove the actual asset because it is simply holding a reference inside a collection. You can have the same asset in multiple collections and create as many collections as you wish.

You can switch to Collections view by clicking the **Switch to the Collections view** button in the Content Browser.

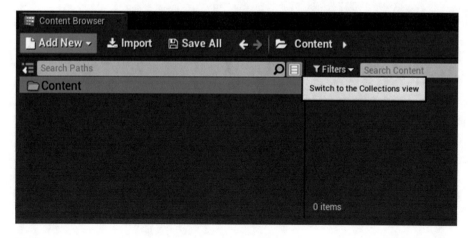

Figure 1-8.

There are three types of collections—Shared, Private, and Local.

- A Shared Collection can be shared with other team members. You must have source control enabled for this option to work.

- A Private Collection can be shared with anyone invited to view the collection. You must have source control enabled for this option to work.

- A Local Collection is only available to you. It is not shared via the network. This option is always available regardless of your source control settings.

Figure 1-9.

After creating a collection, you can drag and drop your assets into it. You can view the number of items available inside a collection.

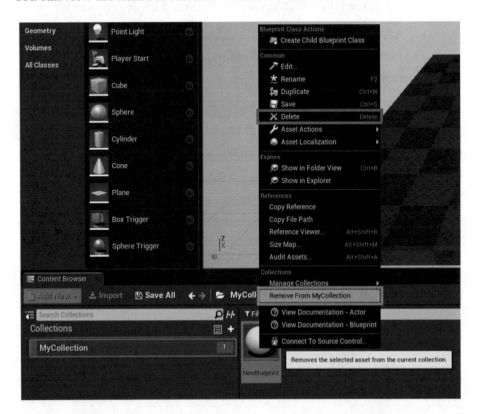

Figure 1-10.

As you can see in Figure 1-10, to remove an asset from a collection, you must first select the collection, right-click the asset, and select **Remove From** *YourCollectionName*. This removes the asset from the collection, but it does *not* delete the asset.

Details

The Details panel contains the selected actor's information and functions. It displays all the transform controls and all the editable properties of the specific actor. All the thumbnails in the Details panel can be double-clicked to open in respective editors. For example, double-clicking a Static Mesh thumbnail opens that mesh. Likewise, if you double-click a material thumbnail, it opens that material in the Material Editor.

The Details panel also offers a search panel that filters properties based on the text. When properties are modified, a small yellow arrow is displayed next to it. This resets the property to its default value.

World Outliner

The World Outliner displays all the actors in the current level. When a Play In Editor session is active, it shows all the actors spawned for the current game in yellow color. You can select any actor in the outliner, and the details panel shows all properties related to that actor. Drag and drop is also supported so you can drag an actor to another to attach it. Searching is also supported with advanced options such as exact match and exclusion.

To exclude an item from search, append - to the search term; for example, *-table* shows everything except for any actor containing the term *table*.

To search for an exact item, append + to the search term; for example, *+table* shows everything with the exact term *table*.

To search for an exact item using the full term, put the term inside double quotes (""); for example, "lunch table" shows everything with the exact term *lunch table.*

Viewport

The viewport is where you spend most of your time developing your game. It is where you see the actual game, so understanding the viewport is crucial for your development. Pressing the G key toggles the viewport between game mode and editor mode. Game mode displays the scene as it appears in the game by hiding all editor-related elements.

In addition to the maximized state of the viewport, Unreal Editor provides an additional state called **Immersive mode,** which is activated by pressing the **F11** shortcut key or accessing the viewport options. When activated, the viewport is maximized to the full extent of the window containing the viewport panel.

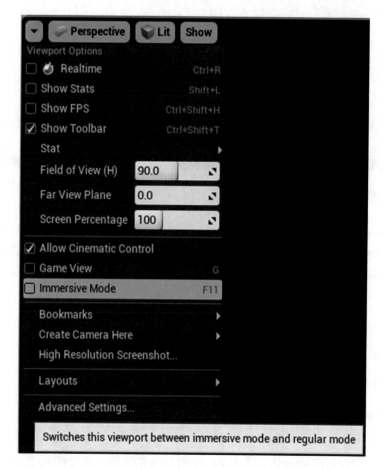

Figure 1-11.

The following explains how to navigate the viewport.

- Right-click and hold the mouse. Use **W**, **A**, **S**, **D** to move around.

- Left-click and hold the mouse. Move your mouse forward, backward, and sideways.

- Hold the middle button on your mouse and move it to pan.

    - Right-click and hold your mouse. Move it to look around.

Knowing these shortcuts can improve your development workflow.

Figure 1-12.

On top of the viewport, you can see the viewport toolbar. It switches to different viewport layouts and view modes, moving/rotating/scaling assets, camera speed, and so forth. You can switch translation modes using the following shortcuts.

- **W** to move the actor

- **E** to rotate the actor

- **R** to scale the actor

Use the **spacebar** to toggle between all three selections.

Note   You can toggle the visibility of this toolbar by pressing **Ctrl+Shift+T**.

At the very end of the toolbar, you see a number icon. This is the camera movement speed inside the editor. You can click it and adjust the slider to the right for faster camera movement or slide it to the left for slower camera movement. To quickly change it, press and hold the right mouse button inside the viewport, and use your mouse wheel to adjust the camera speed. Scroll up for higher speed and scroll down for lower speed.

CHAPTER 2

Introduction to Blueprints

UE4 Blueprints is a visual gameplay scripting language based on a node graph in which you connect nodes from left to right. It can create full-fledged games or simple/complex game mechanics, such as those that open the door to level-wide puzzles. The biggest advantage of Blueprints is that you don't need a programmer to create the logic. Artists can easily make anything they want inside Blueprints and share it with a programmer.

This system is extremely powerful because it offers the artist a full range of tools that are generally only available to programmers. On top of that, C++ programmers can create baseline systems that can be accessed or modified by Blueprint users.

Nodes

In Blueprints (or any other visual programming language), a node is a self-contained functionality that does something unique. In Unreal Engine, Blueprint nodes are objects that can be anything—events, flow control operations, functions, variables, and so on. The source code for the node can be big or small. In Unreal Engine 4, a developer can use C++ to make a Blueprint node, which is accessed in the Graph Editor panel.

Figure 2-1 diagrams the logic done in a node editor to open a door that requires a key.

© Satheesh Pv 2021
S. Pv, *Beginning Unreal Engine 4 Blueprints Visual Scripting*,
https://doi.org/10.1007/978-1-4842-6396-9_2

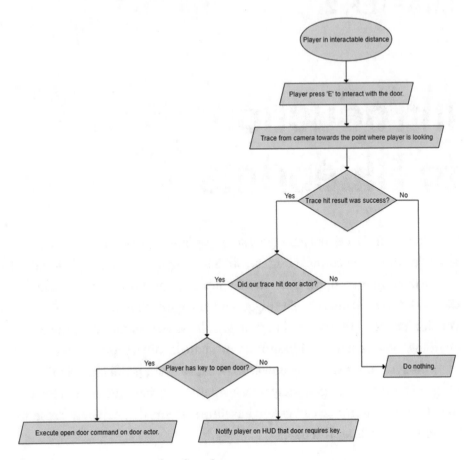

Figure 2-1. *An example of nodes*

Blueprint Types

There are multiple types of Blueprints, which you need to understand to use them efficiently. All Blueprints types (except Level) are created in the Content Browser.

Blueprint Classes

The Blueprint class is the most common type used in your game because it self-contains gameplay mechanics, and it is easily reused across multiple levels. Blueprint classes are inherited from native C++ classes and can have their functionality.

You can create your own C++ classes and mark them as *Blueprintable* to create Blueprint classes. They can interact with each other to create interesting gameplay mechanics; for example, a light Blueprint and a switch Blueprint that communicate to toggle on or off a light. You could also make the switch interact with multiple lights to toggle them on/off randomly or sequentially.

To create a Blueprint class, right-click the Content Browser, and under Create Basic Asset, select Blueprint Class, as shown in Figure 2-2.

Figure 2-2. *Select Blueprint class*

Figure 2-3 shows an example graph with an event that, when triggered, lists all the actors present in the world (the Get All Actors Of Class node), goes through each of them (the For Each Loop node) individually, and calls the toggle light function for each of them.

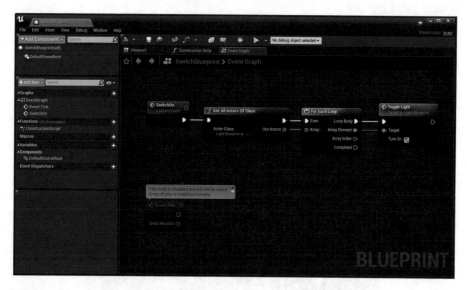

Figure 2-3. *Example Blueprint class with a custom event*

Level Blueprint

A Level Blueprint cannot be created manually but is included within the level itself. It is available when the level is loaded. You can reference any asset in the world and interact with it. If you reference a Blueprint class inside a Level Blueprint, you can access all the public variables and functions in that class.

Note   A public variable or function is accessed from outside the class.

The advantage of using a Level Blueprint is that it is easier to access the actors on the level because you can directly reference them without casting. This is useful when creating events or functions that should be isolated to the level. An example is triggering a cinematic when a certain condition is met.

Figure 2-4 shows how to open a Level Blueprint.

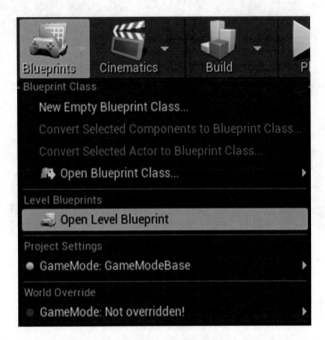

Figure 2-4. *Access Level Blueprint from Editor toolbar*

In a Level Blueprint, you can reference any asset by selecting it and right-clicking (see Figure 2-5).

Figure 2-5. *Referencing an asset*

Blueprint Interface

A Blueprint Interface is a special type of Blueprint in which you can only create functions with their input and output parameters and variables. Let's quickly go over these terms.

- **Functions** are graphs with a single entry pin and a single output pin. Inside it, you can connect any number of nodes that make up your logic so that when the function is called, it starts from the entry pin, activates all the connected nodes, and exits through the output pin. Interfaces cannot contain any function implementation, which means you can only create a function without any logic (graphs are read-only), and variables cannot be created.

- **Variables** are nodes that hold a value or a reference to an object or actor in the world.

27

Interfaces can be added to multiple other Blueprints, and they are guaranteed to contain the functions created in the interface, which can then be implemented. This allows multiple Blueprints to share one common interface; for example, imagine you have two completely different Blueprints, like tree and ice. You can have an interface that contains a damage function and implement this interface in tree and ice. Inside the tree and ice Blueprints, you can implement the damage function that makes the tree burn and the ice melt. If there is no interface, then you must convert (a.k.a cast) the hit actor to each type of actor and call the damage function.

Figure 2-6 is an example diagram that shows the differences between having an interface and not having an interface.

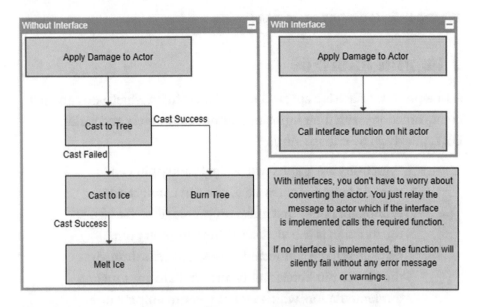

Figure 2-6. *Comparing interface vs. no interface*

To create a Blueprint Interface, right-click the Content Browser, and under Create Advanced Asset, select Blueprint Interface from the Blueprints subsection (see Figure 2-7).

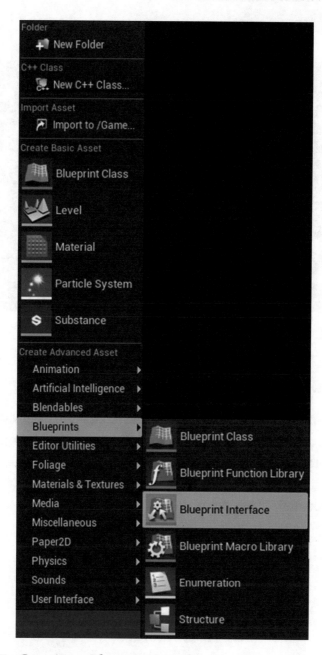

Figure 2-7. *Creating a Blueprint interface*

Figure 2-8 shows the interface after it is created.

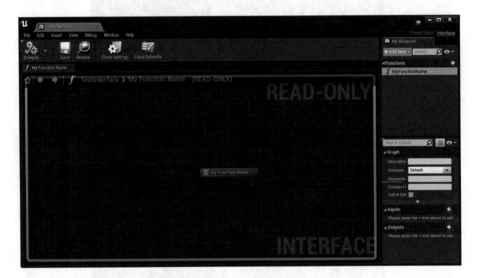

Figure 2-8. *Example Blueprint interface*

Blueprint Macro Library

The Blueprint Macro Library is a Blueprint container that consists of
a collection of graphs placed as nodes in other Blueprints. You cannot
compile a graph in a macro library because it is a container. Any changes
to a macro graph are reflected only when the Blueprint containing that
macro is recompiled (see Figures 2-9 and 2-10).

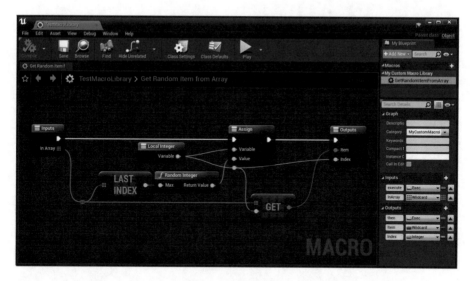

Figure 2-9. *An example macro that gets a random item from an array, which is a list or collection of elements*

Figure 2-10. *An example of how to use the macro in a Blueprint*

Chapter 3 explains how to combine C++ and Blueprints. You can create your own classes and Blueprint-based classes. In addition, you can declare variables and functions in C++ that you can access in Blueprint.

CHAPTER 3

C++ and Unreal Engine 4

C++ is used in Unreal Engine 4 to create gameplay elements or modify the engine. In this chapter, you learn how to install Visual Studio for Unreal Engine. You also learn how to create C++ classes and see how they are structured.

Installing Visual Studio

Before you can write and compile C++ code, you need to have Microsoft Visual Studio (Community Edition or higher) installed on your machine (on macOS, you need Xcode). If you are installing Visual Studio for the first time, make sure to include C++ in your installation (see Figure 3-1).

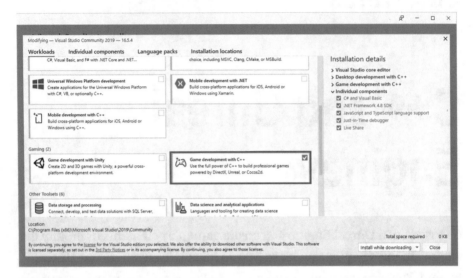

Figure 3-1. *Install Visual Studio with Game Development with C++ enabled*

After the installation, restart your PC. You can start writing C++ in Unreal Engine 4.

Adding C++ Code

You add new C++ classes from Unreal Editor. A C++ class is a user-defined data type that holds its own variables and functions, which are accessed by creating an instance of that class. These variables and functions define the behavior of the class. Class definitions do not take up any memory, but memory is allocated when an instance of the class is created. In UE4, Blueprints extend from one of the classes created in C++ and inherit all the class properties.

In this chapter you create an Actor-based class that can be placed on your level. In Unreal Engine, there are two main classes that you need to be aware of: the Actor class and the Object class. Even though usage depends on your goals, there are some things you must keep in mind when creating classes.

Any Actor-based class can be placed or spawned in the level. These classes have a visual representation and support networking. Object-based classes are generally for storing data, and their memory size is typically smaller than Actor-based classes.

In our Actor-based class, you expose certain properties and functions to Blueprints, which you use to modify the Actor's behavior. To create a new C++ class, click the file menu and select the New C++ Class... option (see Figure 3-2). Alternatively, you can right-click the Content Browser and select New C++ Class. To create a Visual Studio (*.sln) file from the uproject file, right-click the *.uproject file and select Generate Visual Studio project files.

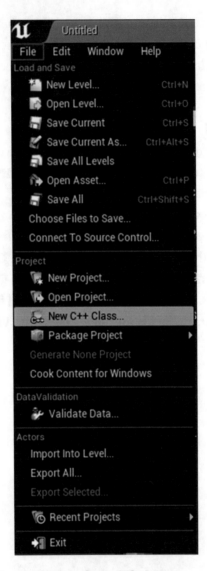

Figure 3-2. *Creating new C++ from File Menu*

You are prompted by a wizard, where you can select the base class. From the list of classes, select the Actor class (see Figure 3-3), and then click Next.

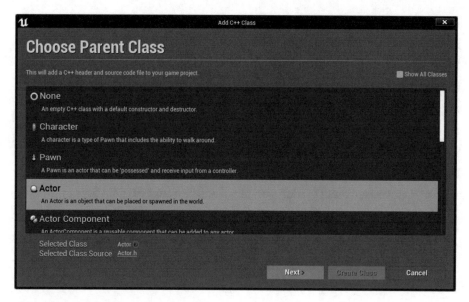

Figure 3-3. *Select Actor class*

The next page prompts you to name your class, enter the location to save to, and chose whether you want to organize your class into a folder structure (see Figure 3-4).

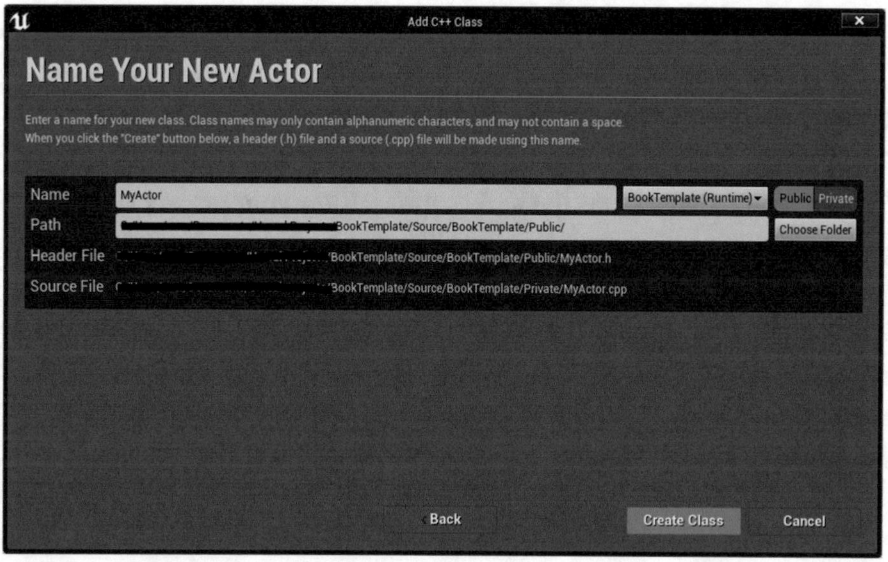

Figure 3-4. *Choose name, location and scope*

Generally, it's a good and recommended practice to arrange your header in a public folder and your source files in a private folder, so select the public option, which puts the header file in the Public folder and the source file in the Private folder. For now, let's stick with the default MyActor name and click Create Class.

Unreal Engine now adds the code to your project and starts compiling C++ code. This might take a few seconds to finish, so you can go to the project folder and see which new folders and files were created.

In your root project folder, you see the following new folders.

- **Binaries**: This folder contains executable files or other files created during compiling. It can be deleted if the Editor is not running and is created next time you compile the project.

- **Intermediate**: This folder contains temporary game object files and Visual Studio–generated project files. It can be deleted safely.

- **Source**: This folder contains your game-specific code files. Obviously, don't delete it.

If you go inside the Source folder, you see that some extra files were created, such as the *YourProjectName*.Target.cs and *YourProjectName.*Build.cs files (the actual name of your project replaces YourProjectName). The Target file determines the build settings (how your project is built) for a specific target (such as Game, Editor, etc.), whereas the build file determines which modules should be built. Modules are containers, including a collection of C++ classes accompanied by a C# build file (with the *.build.cs extension). When you build a module, a corresponding DLL file is generated in the Binaries folder. When you ship your project, all modules are linked together in a single EXE file.

Inside the Public folder, MyActor.h is the header file. Inside the Private folder, MyActor.cpp is the source file. The Header file is where you declare your variables and functions. You implement variables and functions in the Source file.

Examining the Header

Let's analyze the MyActor.h file.

```cpp
#pragma once

#include "CoreMinimal.h"
#include "GameFramework/Actor.h"
#include "MyActor.generated.h"

UCLASS()
class BOOKTEMPLATE_API AMyActor : public AActor
{
    GENERATED_BODY()

public:
    // Sets default values for this actor's properties
    AMyActor();

protected:
    // Called when the game starts or when spawned
    virtual void BeginPlay() override;

public:
    // Called every frame
    virtual void Tick(float DeltaTime) override;

};
```

#pragma once

#pragma once is called a preprocessor directive, which means that you only include this header file once. If you include MyActor.h multiple times in any other file, all subsequent inclusions are ignored.

UCLASS( ) macro

UCLASS() macro is a special macro required by Unreal Engine to make the Editor aware of the class and include it for serialization, optimization, and other Engine-related functionalities. This macro is paired with the GENERATED_BODY() macro, which includes additional functions and type definitions in the class body.

Note   The UCLASS( ) macro can take parameters (a.k.a., Specifiers). You can read more about them at `https://docs.unrealengine.com/en-US/Programming/UnrealArchitecture/Reference/Classes/Specifiers/index.html`.

---

class BOOKTEMPLATE_API AMyActor : public AActor

`class BOOKTEMPLATE_API AMyActor : public AActor` is the beginning of your class. The _API macro is related to DLL linkage, which means it tags functions, classes, or data public to the DLL file; any other module that imports this API module can access these classes or functions directly. This is passed to the compiler from Unreal Build Tool. `public AActor` means that you inherited this class from Actor type. Inheriting is a feature in which you create a new class (also known as a *derived class*) from an existing class (also known as a *base class*). The inherited class derives all the features of its base class (also known as a *parent class*) and can have its own functionality.

In this line, you might have noticed prefixes on class names. Instead of MyActor, it is AMyActor. This is because the Unreal reflection system requires classes to be prefixed by a certain letter. The reflection system is Unreal Engine's foundational technology. It can examine itself at runtime. The following is a list of the prefixes and what each means.

- A for Actor type (e.g., AActor, AController, AGameMode)

- U for Unreal Object (e.g., UObject, UActorComponent, USceneComponent)

- T for Template (e.g., TWeakPtr, TArray, TMap)

- S for Slate (e.g., SWidget, SCompundWidget, SCurveEditor)

- I for Interface (e.g., IAssetRegistry, ILevelViewport, IAsyncTask)

- E for Enum (e.g., EAnchorWidget, EAcceptConnection)

- G for Global (e.g., GEditor, GWorld)

- F for Float (e.g., FVector, FGameplayTag)

public:, protected:, and private:

public:, protected:, and private: are called *access specifiers* (also known as *access modifiers*). They define how variables, functions, and so forth are accessed outside of this class.

- **public**: Any outside class can access members

- **protected**: Any inheriting class can access members

- **private**: No other class can access members

41

AMyActor( )

AMyActor( ) is the constructor, which is a special function that is automatically called when an object is created. It has the same name as the class and never returns any type. It is where you initialize all the default values for any type defined in the header files. For example, if you create a variable with type int32 (like int32 MyVariable;) inside the constructor, you can assign any default value, such as MyVariable = 1.

virtual void BeginPlay( ) override

The override keyword means this function was already declared and defined in the Actor class, and you are overriding it to have your own custom functionality. So, you declare the BeginPlay function that is from the Actor class. The same idea applies to the Tick method.

Examining the Source File

The header file only declares the functions and contains no implementation (the code carries out no actions). Since all implementation is done in the source file (*.cpp), let's look at the source file.

```cpp
#include "MyActor.h"

AMyActor::AMyActor()
{
     PrimaryActorTick.bCanEverTick = true;
}

void AMyActor::BeginPlay()
{
     Super::BeginPlay();
}
```

```
void AMyActor::Tick(float DeltaTime)
{
    Super::Tick(DeltaTime);
}
```

This source file contains only a very basic implementation. Something important to remember here are the Super calls (Super::BeginPlay(); and Super::Tick();), which mean that even when you override these functions, they still call the base implementation defined in the parent class. It is extremely important to include Super calls if you are overriding native engine implementations.

Exposing Variables and Functions to Blueprints

From the C++ class, you can expose the functions or variables that you need to Blueprints so designers can modify them accordingly. You modify the newly added actor to have variables and functions exposed to Blueprints.

Modifying the Header

First, let's add a few variables. Add the following code under the GENERATED_BODY() macro.

```
private:

    /* Our root component for this actor. We can assign a Mesh
    to this component using Mesh variable. */
    UPROPERTY(VisibleAnywhere)
    UStaticMeshComponent* MeshComponent;
```

```
/* Determines if this item can be collected. */
UPROPERTY(EditAnywhere)
bool bCanBeCollected;

/* Just an example to show toggleable option using
metadata specifier. */
UPROPERTY(EditAnywhere, meta = (EditCondition =
"bCanBeCollected"))
int32 ToggleableOption;
```

- UCLASS macros are for classes.

- UPROPERTY macros are for variables.

- UFUNCTION macros are for functions.

UPROPERTY is a special engine macro. Inside, you specify how to expose your variable.

Here are some of the common specifiers for UPROPERTY.

- **EditAnywhere**: This property can be edited in default Blueprint and the instances placed in the world.

- **EditDefaultsOnly**: This property can be edited in default Blueprint only. When you place the instances of an actor in the world, you cannot edit this property individually by instance.

- **EditInstanceOnly**: This property can only be changed for instances placed in the level. This property is not available in default Blueprint.

- **VisibleAnywhere**: This property has the same visibility as EditAnywhere, but the property cannot be edited. It is read-only.

- **VisibleDefaultsOnly**: This property has the same visibility as EditDefaultsOnly, but the property cannot be edited. It is read-only.

- **VisibleInstanceOnly**: This property has the same visibility as EditInstanceOnly, but the property cannot be edited. It is read-only.

If necessary, property editing can be enabled or disabled based on boolean values. This is achieved using a metadata specifier called EditCondition. An example is provided in the preceding code.

Underneath AMyActor();, add a function that is exposed to the Blueprint.

```
/* Just a sample Blueprint exposed function. This comment
appears as a tooltip in Blueprint Graph. */
UFUNCTION(BlueprintCallable, Category = "My Actor")
void CollectMe(bool bDestroy = true);
```

Modifying the Source File

Now let's modify the source file. First, you need to assign a Mesh Component variable, which is a Static Mesh Component type used to create an instance of Static Mesh. You do this because you need a valid root component to move this actor in the world. To do that, you need to construct the Static Mesh Component object inside the constructor and assign it there. Let's look at the following example code.

```
MeshComponent = CreateDefaultSubobject<UStaticMeshComponent>
(TEXT("MeshComponent"));
RootComponent = MeshComponent;
```

In the code, you see a special Engine function called CreateDefaultSubobject. This function allows you to create an object of the given type, which is visible in the Editor. This function can only be called inside constructors; calling it at runtime crashes the Editor.

Then create a definition for the CollectMe function inside the source file.

Note   Function names can be anything, but generally, it is recommended that they are verbs that describe the function's usage or are based on the return value.

For now, you log information based on the input parameter and the bCanBeCollected variable. Define the function as follows.

```cpp
void AMyActor::CollectMe(bool bDestroy /*= true*/)
{
    // Check if this actor can be collected...
    if (bCanBeCollected)
    {
        // ...Now check if the actor must be destroyed...
        if (bDestroy)
        {
            // ...Actor has to be destroyed so log that
            information and destroy.
            UE_LOG(LogTemp, Log, TEXT("Actor collected and
            destroyed."));
            Destroy();
        }
        else
        {
            // ...Dont destroy the actor. Just log the
            information.
            UE_LOG(LogTemp, Warning, TEXT("Actor collected
            but not destroyed."));
        }
    }
}
```

```
    else
    {
        // ...Actor cannot be collected thus cannot be
        destroyed.
        UE_LOG(LogTemp, Error, TEXT("Actor not collected."));
    }
}
```

The Final Code

The entire header should look like the following code. Note that the BeginPlay and Tick functions have been removed.

```
#pragma once

#include "CoreMinimal.h"
#include "GameFramework/Actor.h"
#include "MyActor.generated.h"

UCLASS()
class BOOKTEMPLATE_API AMyActor : public AActor
{
    GENERATED_BODY()

private:

    /* Our root component for this actor. We can assign a Mesh
    to this component using Mesh variable. */
    UPROPERTY(VisibleAnywhere)
    UStaticMeshComponent* MeshComponent;

    /* Determines if this item can be collected. */
    UPROPERTY(EditAnywhere)
    bool bCanBeCollected;
```

```
    /* Just an example to show toggleable option using
    metadata specifier. Uncheck Can Be Collected boolean and
    this option  disable (grey out). */
    UPROPERTY(EditAnywhere, meta = (EditCondition =
    "bCanBeCollected"))
    int32 ToggleableOption;

public:

    AMyActor();

    /* Collect this actor. Blueprint exposed example function.
    This also acts as a tooltip in Blueprint Graph. */
    UFUNCTION(BlueprintCallable, Category = "My Actor")
    void CollectMe(bool bDestroy = true);

};
```

And the source code should look like this.

```
#include "MyActor.h"
#include "Components/StaticMeshComponent.h"

AMyActor::AMyActor()
{
    MeshComponent = CreateDefaultSubobject<UStaticMesh
    Component>(TEXT("MeshComponent"));
    RootComponent = MeshComponent;

    bCanBeCollected = true;
    ToggleableOption = 0;

    // Set this actor to call Tick() every frame. You can turn
        this off to improve performance if you don't need it.
    PrimaryActorTick.bCanEverTick = true;

}
```

```cpp
void AMyActor::CollectMe(bool bDestroy /*= true*/)
{
    // Check if this actor can be collected...
    if (bCanBeCollected)
    {
        // ...Now check if the actor must be destroyed...
        if (bDestroy)
        {
            // ...Actor has to be destroyed so log that
            information and destroy.
            UE_LOG(LogTemp, Log, TEXT("Actor collected and
            destroyed."));
            Destroy();
        }
        else
        {
            // ...Dont destroy the actor. Just log a warning.
            UE_LOG(LogTemp, Warning, TEXT("Actor collected
            but not destroyed."));
        }
    }
    else
    {
        // ...Actor cannot be collected thus cannot be
        destroyed. Log as an error.
        UE_LOG(LogTemp, Error, TEXT("Actor not collected."));
    }
}
```

Using the Class

In Visual Studio, press F5 to compile and launch the project. Once the Editor is up and running, right-click the Content Browser and select Blueprint Class. In the Pick Parent Class window, expand all the classes and search for My Actor. You should then pick our custom Actor class as a base for Blueprint (see Figure 3-5).

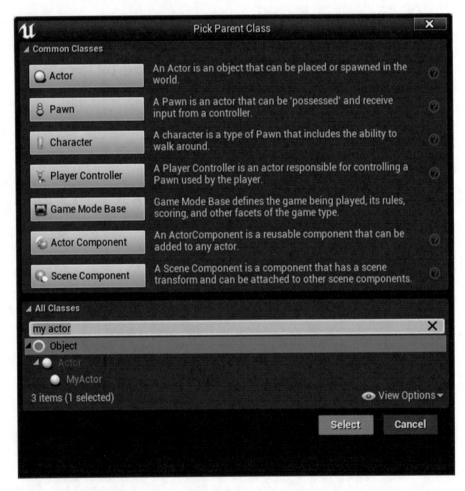

Figure 3-5. *Select our previously created C++ class as parent*

Next, open the Blueprint Actor. You can assign your custom mesh and adjust the properties you chose to expose to Blueprint (see Figure 3-6). Hovering your mouse over the properties shows the comment you added in C++ as a tooltip.

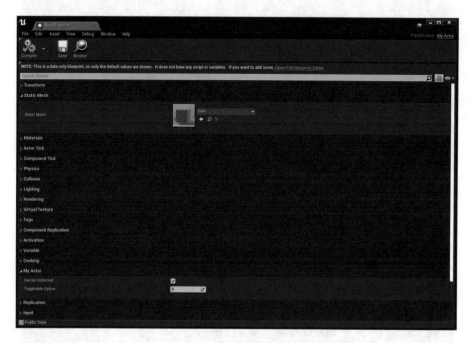

Figure 3-6. *Adjust properties exposed from C++*

Calling C++ Functions in Blueprints

My Actor Blueprint is ready in the Editor. You also made a Blueprint Callable function inside the actor called Collect Me. In this section, we use relatively simple logic to quickly call this function in the Level Blueprint.

First, drag and drop the newly created My Actor Blueprint onto the level. After that, make sure My Actor Blueprint is selected in the Level Editor and open Level Blueprint. Inside Level Blueprint, right-click the graph and create a reference to the selected My Actor Blueprint. In Figure 3-7, I placed My Actor Blueprint on the level, selected it, and created a reference in Level Blueprint.

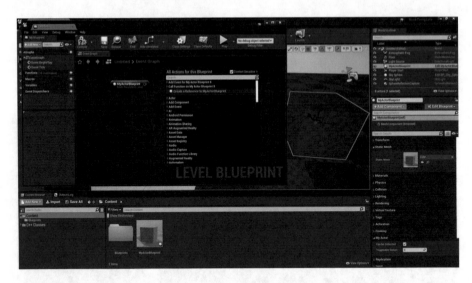

Figure 3-7. *Referencing My Actor Blueprint*

From the reference, drag a pin and select the Collect Me function (see Figure 3-8).

Figure 3-8. *Calling Collect Me function*

Now you can call the Collect Me function any time you want. As an example, let's call it in Begin Play after a two-second delay. The final graph looks like Figure 3-9.

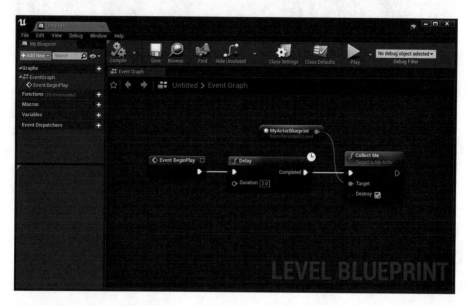

Figure 3-9. *Final Graph*

Even though you only used a boolean as an input here, you can use other types, like floats, integers, units, and even UObjects or AActors. For example, if you want to use int32, change the boolean to int32 in both the header and source files. Void CollectMe(int32 MyIntVariable);. After that, you can use MyIntVariable in the CollectMe function defined in the source file.

Click the Play button. After 2 seconds, the My Actor Blueprint prints the message (see Figure 3-10) to log as defined in C++ and destroys itself.

Figure 3-10. *Logged information displayed*

CHAPTER 4

Gameplay Classes

This chapter looks at some of the important and common gameplay classes you use in almost all projects.

Actor

The Actor class is the base for all placeable and spawnable objects in a game world. Anything that can be dragged and dropped into the world or spawned at runtime is inherited from the Actor class. Actor classes are basic classes that can support translation (position), rotation, and scale (size). Actors can contain any number of Actor Component classes that define how it should move and render. By default, Actors are generic classes and do not have any kind of visual representation. It is up to the component to give it a visual representation. Actor classes also support replication and function calls across the network.

Game Mode Base

Game Mode Base defines the basic rules for your game, such as which actors are allowed, player scores, winning rules, and so forth. It holds information about all the players in the game world. For example, you can define the score required to win a match. Game Mode sets the classes for Pawn, Player Controller, Game State, Player State, Spectator, and more. In a multiplayer game, the Game Mode class only exists on the server, and for the client, it is always null, as if it never exists. This is only applicable to multiplayer games because, in single-player games, there are no clients, only the server.

Game Mode, a subclass of Game Mode Base, is designed toward multiplayer games. It contains default behavior for picking spawn points for each player.

Game State Base

Game State Base defines the current state of the game. Game State classes are spawned by the Game Mode. They are particularly useful in a multiplayer game because Game State classes are replicated to every client, so any change that happens to a replicated value reflects all clients. For example, imagine you have a game mode that requires some number of kills to win the game. Every time the player eliminates another player, it runs a server function that updates the current number of total kills in Game Mode, which is then changed in the game state, and it is updated on all clients. Game State is a subclass of Game State Base.

Game Instance

The Game Instance class is created when you run the game. It exists when the game is running. It is useful for transferring information between levels. For example, imagine in your game that the player finishes a certain challenge. You can store this specific information in Game Instance. When the player returns to the main menu, you can show a message on the screen that says the challenge has been completed. Game Instance is a UObject-based class; it is not replicated to anyone. The server or client is not aware of any other game instances other than their own.

Game Instance is set via Project Settings ➤ Maps & Modes ➤ Game Instance class (see Figure 4-1).

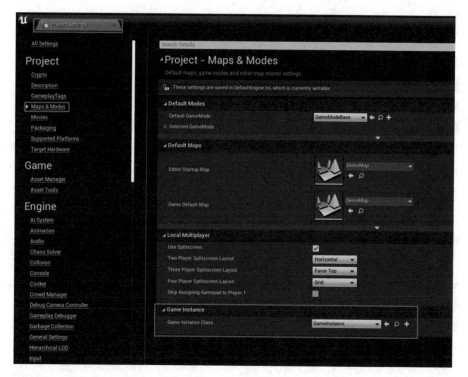

Figure 4-1. *Setting Game Instance class*

The following describes the three main Game classes.

- **Game Mode** holds authority of the game flow and only exists on the server, which prevents cheating.

- **Game State** holds the replicated state of the game. It exists on the server and client. Clients can ask the Game State about the current state of the game, and the server can modify the current state of the game, which is replicated to all clients.

- **Game Instance** is a true persistent class that is guaranteed to be available and accessible from the very beginning of your game until you exit. It is not replicated and exists on both the server and client.

Pawn

Pawn is an Actor-based class that acts as a physical representation of a player or artificial intelligence (AI). Pawns are controlled by a Controller, which is either a Player Controller or an AI Controller. Even though the pawn does not have visual representation by default, it still represents location, rotation, and so forth, within the game world. Pawns can contain their own movement logic, but it's better done in the Controller. Pawns can be replicated across the network.

Character

Character is extended from the Pawn class to support visual representation by using the Skeletal Mesh Component for animations. It also includes the Capsule Component to simulate movement collisions, and the Character Movement Component, a feature-rich component that includes movements such as walk, run, jump, swim, and fly. It also includes basic networking support, which makes it a first-class choice for bipedal characters. The Character Movement Component is specific to the Character class, so it cannot be used in any other class.

Player Controller

Player Controllers are subclassed from the Controller, which is essentially the brain of the Pawn it is controlling. Based on the context, the Controller is a Player Controller if it is controlled by a human player (and can handle all player inputs) or an AI Controller is controlled by artificial intelligence.

By default, a Controller can only control one Pawn at any given time by calling the Possess() function. It stops controlling by calling the UnPossess() function. A Controller also allows notifications from the Pawn class that it is controlling. In a networked game, the server is aware of all controllers while the client is only aware of its own local controller.

Player State

Player State is a replicated Actor that is available for every player. There is only one player state in a single-player game, but in a multiplayer game, each player has their own player state. Since it is replicated, the server and client are aware of all player states, and all of them can be accessed from the Game State class. This is a good place to store network-relevant information about a player, like score, player name, and so forth.

Let's share a scenario where you can use these classes. When writing this book, battle royale games (*Fortnite*, *PUBG*, etc.) are very popular among us gamers, so if you were to create a battle royale game, you could use the following classes.

- **Game Mode**: This class defines the rules. In this class, you track the number of players that have entered the match, the number that are alive, the number that are dead, and the quitters. This class also tracks and decides other game elements, such as a battle plane (or a battle bus in *Fortnite*), circle, and so on, and whether the match has started or is waiting to start (warm up).

- **Game State**: This class tracks the replicated state of the game. For example, when the game mode transitions from prematch (lobby) to a match state (battle plane or bus starting on top of the map), it notifies the game state that the state has changed, and the game state can notify all the clients that match started.

- **Game Instance**: This class saves information about any objectives or challenges completed in the game so that the player can be rewarded when they return to the main menu.

- **Character**: The visual representation of the character.

- **Pawn**: A vehicle or an animal in your game. (Optional)

- **Player Controller**: This class handles all the input
  and creates and manages the user interfaces. It can
  also send RPCs (remote procedure calls) to the server.
  The server is aware of all player controllers (e.g., if the
  game has 100 players, the server knows all 100 player
  controllers), but the client is only aware of its own.

- **Player State**: This class holds the information related
  to player-specific states (e.g., the number of players you
  killed, the amount of ammo you fired, and so forth).

Creating Character Class and Player Controller Class

In this section, you learn how to create a new character class that allows
the player to move around in the game world using the Player Controller
class. Later in this section, a UMG (Unreal Motion Graphics) widget shows
health information to the player.

To create a new character class, right-click the Content Browser
and select Blueprint Class. You are prompted to pick a parent class for
your Blueprint. Select Character from the Common Classes section (see
Figure 4-2).

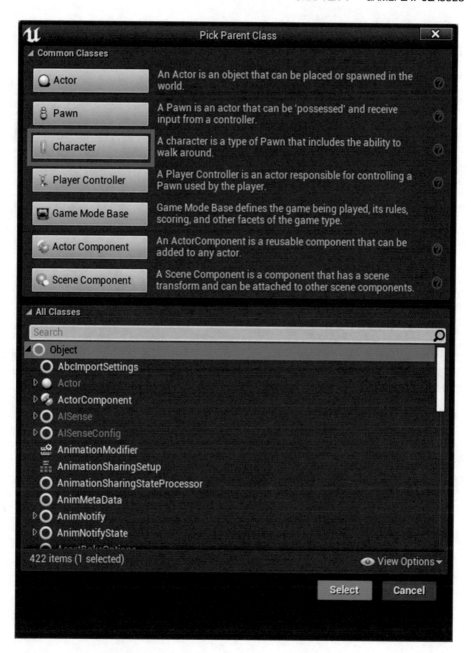

Figure 4-2. *Selecting character class*

Next, open the Character Blueprint. You see the default Capsule Component, Mesh Component, and Character Movement Component (see Figure 4-3).

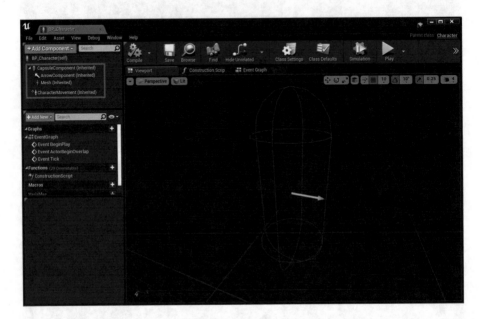

Figure 4-3. Default components

- **CapsuleComponent** is the actor's root component. It is responsible for collisions. CharacterMovement is aware of this capsule component and moves it around according to the player input.

- **ArrowComponent** is an editor-only component that helps indicate which direction the object is facing.

- **Mesh** is the visual representation of the character and is of the Skeletal Mesh Component type.

- **CharacterMovement** handles the movement logic of the associated character. This component updates the location and rotation of CapsuleComponent, which makes the character move. It is a highly featured component and includes network support.

We will use the default Mannequin that comes with the Engine as our character. To use it, you must add the Third Person Project to your project. If not yet added, you can do it by clicking the Add New button in the Content Browser and selecting **Add Feature or Content Pack** (see Figure 4-4).

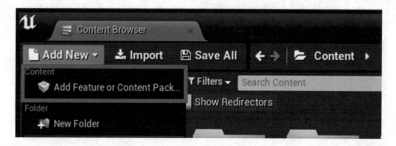

Figure 4-4. *Adding feature pack or starter content from Content Browser*

Next, select Third Person from the Blueprint Feature tab and click Add To Project. Now you have the Mannequin. Assign the Mannequin to the previously created Character Blueprint class.

You may notice that the mesh is not aligned properly. The character mesh is at the center of the Capsule Component, and the rotation of the character is facing in the wrong direction. To fix this, adjust the location and rotation of the Mesh Component to the proper values.

- Location: X: 0, Y: 0, Z: –97

- Rotation: Roll: 0, Pitch: 0, Yaw: 270

You also need to add a camera to the player to have a proper view. First, you add a Spring Arm Component, which maintains its children at a fixed distance from its parent. To do this, click the Add Component button in the Components tab and select Spring Arm under the Camera section (see Figure 4-5).

Figure 4-5. Add spring arm component

Using the same method, add a Camera to the Spring Arm Component. The result should look like Figure 4-6.

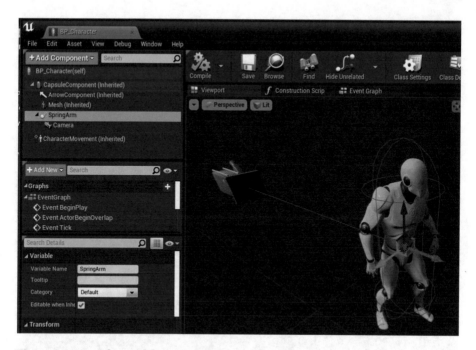

Figure 4-6. *After adding Camera to Spring arm*

If you drag and drop the character into the Level Editor, you can preview how the player sees the character from this camera angle. There are few settings to change in the Character class. Click the Class Defaults button in the Blueprint Editor toolbar. In the Details panel, disable Use Controller Rotation Yaw under the Pawn section. After that, select the Spring Arm Component that you added and enable Use Pawn Control Rotation under Camera Settings. Finally, select the Character Movement Component and enable Orient Rotation to Movement.

Now that our character is almost ready, let's implement a basic function that moves it around.

First, you need to add two functions that make the character move forward/backward and left/right. To create a new function, click the Function button under the Functions section in the My Blueprint tab in your Character class. After you click the button, you can rename the function; let's call it **Move Forward or Backward**.

You also add a float parameter called ScaleValue, which scales the input. To add a parameter to the function, select the purple node, and in the Details panel, add a new input parameter and select Float from the drop-down list (see Figure 4-7).

Figure 4-7. Adding input to function

Inside this function, you get the character's control rotation. You use its yaw rotation to find the forward vector, which you use as the direction to move the character. The forward vector is a normalized vector that points in the direction that the actor is facing. The final function should look like what's shown in Figure 4-8.

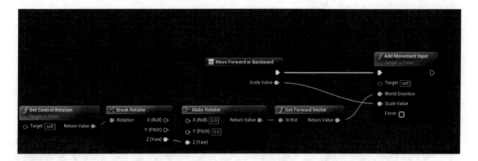

Figure 4-8. *Final function*

The same function can be duplicated; call it **Move Left or Right**. Rather than the Get Forward Vector, use the Get Right Vector. The final function should look like Figure 4-9.

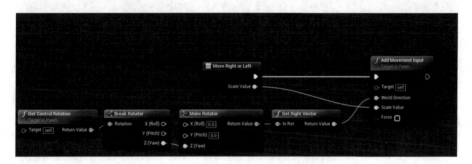

Figure 4-9. *Same function with Get Right Vector*

Note that the two functions look the same except for Get Forward Vector and Get Right Vector.

Before continuing with input, you need to define these functions in Input Settings under the Engine section, which is accessed from Project Settings. In Figure 4-10, you see the basic input settings that I defined.

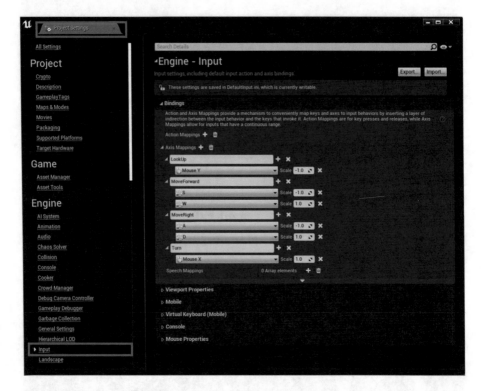

Figure 4-10. *Adding inputs via Project settings*

The axis values can be accessed from a Pawn class or Controller class. We will use the latter option.

To create a new player controller, right-click Content Browser, and select Blueprint Class. In the next window, select Player Controller and open the asset to add nodes. Inside the Player Controller graph, right-click the graph and search for MoveForward, which is the same name you defined in Input settings. Once you select the node, right-click the graph again and search for Get Controlled Pawn. The return value of the Get Controlled Pawn node points to the current character or pawn the player is controlling. So from the return value, drag a pin and cast it to the Character class that you created. From the Casted Character class, drag another pin and call the Move Forward or Backward function you created. Connect this set of nodes to the InputAxis MoveForward event. The same set of nodes connect to the InputAxis MoveRight event, but instead of using the Move Forward or Backward function, you call the Move Right or Left function. The final graph should look like Figure 4-11.

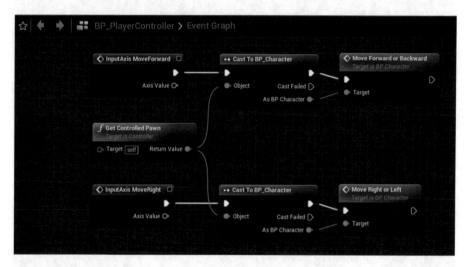

Figure 4-11. *Final graph with all functions*

The last step uses the Character and Controller classes in our game. To do so, create a new Game Mode Blueprint and assign our character as the default pawn and the controller as our Player Controller class in Game Mode. In Figure 4-12, you can see I assigned our Blueprint-created character and controller to the Game Mode class.

Figure 4-12. *Assign controller and pawn in game mode*

To use BP_GameMode we created, you need to assign this to your level's World Settings. In your Level Editor's main toolbar, click Settings and select World Settings (see Figure 4-13).

Figure 4-13. *Select world settings from settings*

In the World Settings tab, assign the game mode (see Figure 4-14).

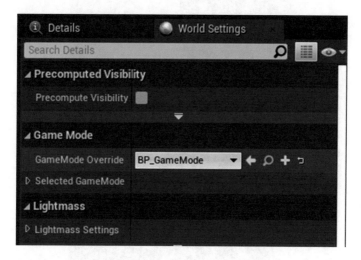

Figure 4-14. *Assign game mode*

If you press Play, you can move the character around using the W, A, S, D keys, or any keys you assigned in Input Settings.

Creating and Showing Data on HUD

In this section, you add a basic HUD to the player character, create a health variable that changes when the player takes damage, and create a welcome text that automatically disappears after 3 seconds. Note that the implementation shown here only works in single-player games; it does not work in multiplayer games.

First, let's create a UMG widget Blueprint by right-clicking the Content Browser and selecting User Interface ➤ Widget Blueprint (see Figure 4-15).

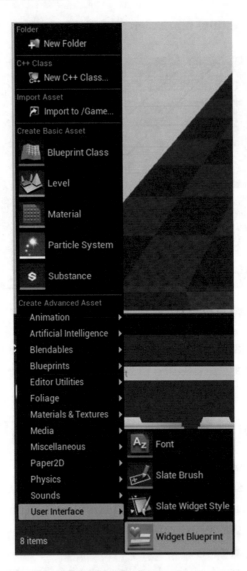

Figure 4-15. *Creating widget blueprint*

Open the Widget Blueprint. You see the main Designer section, where you drag and drop different widgets from the Palette panel. In the top-right corner, you can switch between Designer view and Graph view (see Figure 4-16). Graph view is used to create all the Blueprint logic.

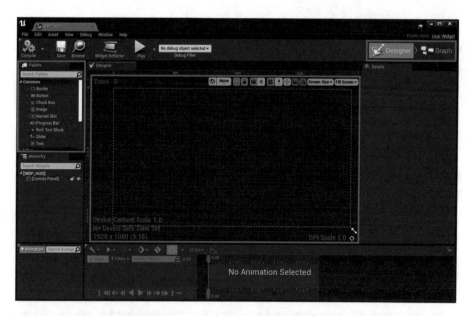

Figure 4-16. *UMG layout*

Let's drag and drop a progress bar widget from the palette to the Designer tab. Select the progress bar widget. In the Details panel, enter a name for the progress bar (e.g., HealthBar)(see Figure 4-17).

Figure 4-17. *Setting variable name*

73

To implement the logic, let's first switch to the Graph view and create a new event. Right-click inside the graph and select Add New Event from the Add Event category. Rename this event to UpdateHealth and add two float parameters called CurrentHealth and MaxHealth. Drag from the CurrentHealth float pin, search for the Divide operator, and select it. Then connect MaxHealth to the B input of Divide. This is the result that you use in ProgressBar. It is done because ProgressBar works in the 0–1 range, and since you are dividing CurrentHealth by MaxHealth, you get the result in this range.

To set the value of ProgressBar, drag and drop ProgressBar from the Variables category to the Graph view, drag from the pin, and search for Set Percent. Connect the result of the Divide node to the In Percent of Set Percent node. Your node setup should look similar to Figure 4-18.

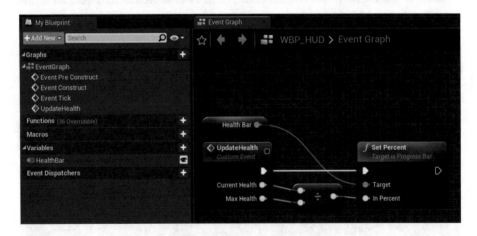

Figure 4-18. *Update health setup*

To use of widget, you need to add it to the screen. Let's open the Character Blueprint and switch to Event Graph. Right-click inside the graph and search for the Create Widget node. Inside the Class input, set the newly created UMG HUD. Then right-click Return Value and choose Promote To Variable (see Figure 4-19). Name it **PlayerHUD**. This caches the result to a variable so that you can access it anytime you want.

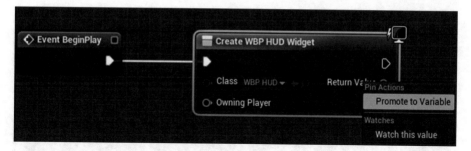

Figure 4-19. *Promoting to variable*

From the PlayerHUD variable, drag a pin, search for Add To Viewport, and select it (see Figure 4-20).

Figure 4-20. *Adding widget to viewport*

If you play now, you can see the newly added HUD on your screen, but it does nothing yet because we have not called the Update Health event. To quickly fix this, drag a pin from the PlayerHUD variable and search for UpdateHealth. Now create a float variable called Health, and set its default value to 100. Drag this variable from the My Blueprint tab, connect it to the Current Health of Update Health function, and set Max Health to 100 (see Figure 4-21).

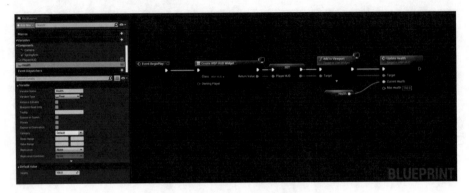

Figure 4-21. *Calling update health event initially*

Once you have set up everything, add the welcome text. Drag and drop the Text widget from the Palette tab to the designer. To align this text in the center of the screen, set the Anchor to center by expanding it and setting both Minimum and Maximum to 0.5. You need to set the alignment to 0.5 also. After that, set Position X and Position Y to 0. The text is now centered on the screen. Next, enable Size To Content to automatically size the widget according to the text.

Under the Content category, change the text to your liking. For this example, let's write something like **Welcome to UMG**. Expand the font under Appearance and set Size to 48. You need the text to disappear after 3 seconds. To do so, make sure that the Is Variable in the Details tab is set to True and enter a name for your Widget (e.g., WelcomeText) (see Figure 4-22).

Figure 4-22. *Setting variable name for text*

Switch to Graph view, and you now can drag and drop the WelcomeText widget from the MyBlueprint tab (under the Variables section) to the graph. Right-click the graph, search for Delay, and select it. Connect the Delay node to Event Construct. Then drag a wire from the output pin of Widget Text, search for Set Visibility, and select it. Change In Visibility from Visible to Collapsed, and connect the output Completed of Delay node to the Set Visibility node. Finally, change the duration of the Delay node to 3 seconds (see Figure 4-23).

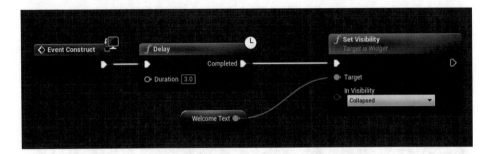

Figure 4-23. *Graph with delay node*

Click the Play button. You see that the welcome text and progress bar are showing (see Figure 4-24).

Figure 4-24. *Playing game with UMG widget added*

Whenever your player is taking damage, you can reduce your health and call Update Health with Health connected to Current Health, which properly updates the progress bar in UMG.

CHAPTER 5

Physics and Raycasting

Physics in Unreal Engine is responsible for the simulation and collision of all physical actors, which means any motion, like falling or applying a force or interaction between them is done using physics. At the time of this book was written, Unreal used PhysX version 3.4, which was used for all simulations.

UE4 includes a built-in high-performance custom physics engine called Chaos Physics Engine, which (at the time of writing this book) is only available through the GitHub source. Chaos Physics is expected to be production-ready in UE4 version 4.26.

Raycasting (also known as *trace*) is the process of sending an invisible ray from one location to another location in the game world and determining if the ray hit anything. The hit result contains information that you can use to alter the game state.

In this chapter, you learn about Simulation, Collision, and Trace.

Simulation

When an object is falling or moved by applying some force, then that object is simulating physics. For physics to simulate, the mesh must have a collision shape first. Because the actual 3D mesh can be complicated, UE4

© Satheesh Pv 2021
S. Pv, *Beginning Unreal Engine 4 Blueprints Visual Scripting*,
https://doi.org/10.1007/978-1-4842-6396-9_5

uses simple proxy shapes, which are called Physics Bodies (also known as BodyInstances), such as a box, sphere, capsule, or custom convex hull to simulate physics. The properties for this physical body are adjusted by selecting the mesh on which you want to apply physics. For example, in Chapter 3, we assigned a Static Mesh Component and created a Blueprint class for our C++ actor.

1. Open the Blueprint and select MeshComponent (Inherited) from the Components tab (see Figure 5-1).

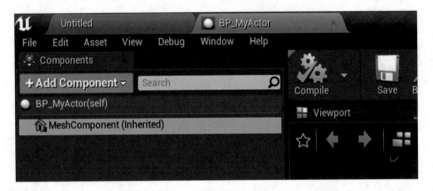

Figure 5-1. *Inherited Mesh Component*

2. In the Details panel, scroll down to the Physics category (see Figure 5-2).

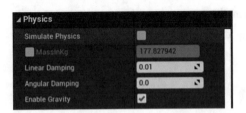

Figure 5-2. *Physics category in details panel*

Let's look at these properties.

- **Simulate Physics**: Enables or disables physics simulation. If this option is grayed-out, you don't have a collision set up on the selected mesh. For Skeletal Mesh, you need a physics asset setup, and for Static Mesh, you need a simple collision setup.

- **MassInKg**: The mass of the object in kilograms.

- **Linear Damping**: The drag force applied to a linear movement, which determines the movement in a straight line.

- **Angular Damping**: The drag force applied to an angular movement, which is the rotational equivalent of linear movement.

- **Enable Gravity**: Determines if the physics simulation should have the force of gravity applied.

Collision

In Unreal, every object with Collision is assigned an object type, which defines how it interacts with other object types. Some object types can block, some can overlap, and others can ignore. An object can also define how it should react to traces using trace channels. By default, there are two types of trace channels: Visibility and Camera.

There are two types of collisions: Blocking and Overlaps.

- **Blocking collisions** occurs when two objects collide and cannot pass through (e.g., an object hitting a wall).

- **Overlap collisions** occur when two objects overlap each other (e.g., an object falling into water).

Collisions are determined by the preset on the component under the Collision category. Collisions generate events with information, including with whom the collision occurred. Figure 5-3 shows the Collision properties.

Figure 5-3. Collision properties of static mesh

- **Simulation Generates Hit Events**: If true, this physics body calls a native On Component Hit event when a collision is a success.

- **Phys Material Override**: Assign a physics material (not to be confused with the material in the next chapter) to define properties such as Friction, Restitution, and Density.

- **Generate Overlap Events**: If true, this physics body calls a native On Begin Overlap event when the overlap starts and calls an On End Overlap event when overlapping ends.

- **Can Character Step Up On**: Determines if the player character can step onto this object. If No, the player is rejected if they try to step on it.

Collision has four different states.

- **No Collision**: There is no representation for any type of collision. This means no overlapping or blocking.

- **Query only**: The object can only trigger overlap events, and no rigid body collisions; the object cannot block any other objects.

- **Physics only**: The object can interact with other objects but does not support overlaps.

- **Collision enabled**: The object can overlap and block other objects.

Let's now look at defining a new trace type and using it in the game to pick up an item.

Using Trace (Raycast) to Pick up an Item

When you want to pick up an item in a game, you look at the item first and press a specific key. When you press that key, under the hood, the Engine sends an invisible ray from the camera location with a specified length. In between the start location and the end location, if the trace hits an object, it returns a hit result containing hit information. Figure 5-4 illustrates how trace works.

Figure 5-4. *Example showing how trace works*

So how does the trace know what to hit? It is done using a trace channel. Unreal Engine comes with two trace channels: Visibility and Camera. In this section, you create our own trace channel, set it to an item, and use trace to detect it.

First and foremost, let's create a trace channel. Open Project Settings by clicking Edit on the menu bar, and then select Project Settings (see Figure 5-5).

Figure 5-5. *Accessing Project settings*

From the Project Settings, click Collision under the Engine section to modify the collision settings (see Figure 5-6).

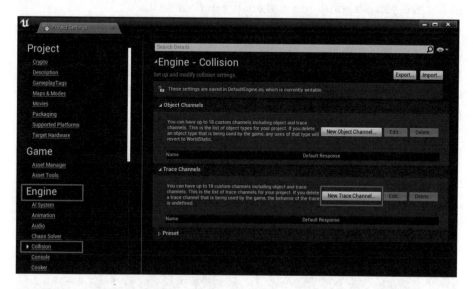

Figure 5-6. *Adding new Trace channel*

Click the New Trace Channel button under the Trace Channels category. A new dialog box appears, prompting you to name the trace and a default response. Enter the name as **MyItemTrace** and set the default response to ignore (see Figure 5-7).

Figure 5-7. *Defining new trace with name and response*

After pressing the Accept button, you see your newly created trace under the Trace Channels category. You can now access this trace channel under every mesh component to enable or disable it.

Before we do anything else, let's first make sure the mesh you are using (1M_Cube) has collision available. Go to the Content Browser where the mesh is located, and hover your mouse over the mesh. In the tooltip, if the Collision Prims is greater than 0, then the mesh has collision included (see Figure 5-8).

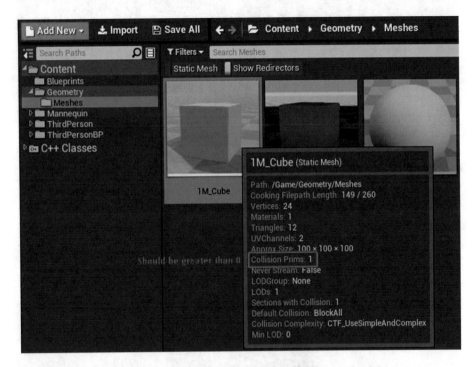

Figure 5-8. *Tool tip showing number of collision primitives*

If the mesh is a missing collision, you can generate a collision shape inside the Static Mesh Editor. From the menu bar, click Collision and select an option to generate your desired collision shape. For simple shapes, you can choose box, cylinder, sphere, or so forth, but for complex shapes, select Auto Convex Collision (see Figure 5-9).

Figure 5-9. *Various collisions*

To use the trace channel, you first open your previously created
Blueprint Actor and select the MeshComponent (inherited) from the
Components tab. Assign the Collision that includes Static Mesh. In our
case, you use the 1M_Cube static mesh.

Next, go to the Details panel and scroll down to the Collision category.
Expand the Collision Presets section and click the BlockAllDynamic drop-
down button. From the list of options, select Custom. By selecting Custom,
you can choose how the object responds to collisions with other objects.
Choose to block the MyItemTrace trace response by enabling Block (see
Figure 5-10).

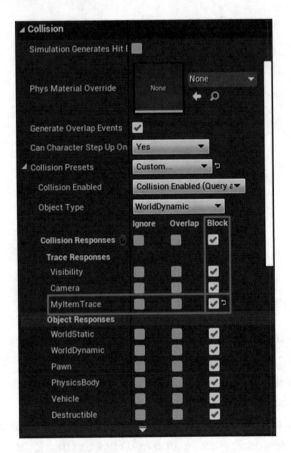

Figure 5-10. *Setting our trace to block*

You have now finished the item setup, but what about trace? You do it in the Character class, but you need to have an input to start the trace. To do that, click Edit on the menu bar and select Project Settings. Next, select Input under the Engine section. On the right , click the + button next to Action Mapping. Name the input anything you want, and select a key for it. I named it Trace and chose E for the key (see Figure 5-11).

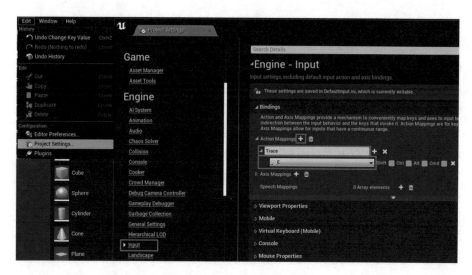

Figure 5-11. *Creating new input to trace*

If you have not added a third-person project, you can do so by clicking the green Add New button in the Content Browser. Select either Add Feature or Content Pack. In the dialog, select Third Person and click **+Add to Project**.

Next, press **Shift+Alt+O** to open the Open Asset dialog. Search for ThirdPersonCharacter and open it. Alternatively, you can navigate to Content/ThirdPerson/Blueprints and open ThirdPersonCharacter Blueprint (see Figure 5-12).

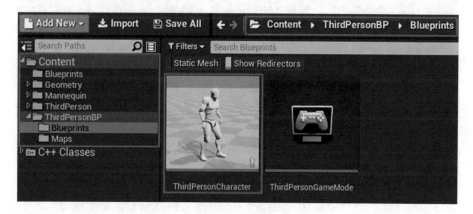

Figure 5-12. *Open third person character*

In the Event graph, right-click and search for Input Trace (it is under Input → Action Events). You can add the Trace event, which is invoked when you press the E key. Right-click again on the graph and search for Line Trace By Channel. (There are other types of traces as well, like Box, Capsule, and Sphere. Read more about them at https://docs.unrealengine. com/en-US/Engine/Physics/Tracing/Overview/index.html).

Line Trace By Channel is the primary node that does the tracing from the start location to the end location. Figure 5-4 illustrates where the trace starts from the Camera and shoots to the direction the Camera is facing. To create that setup, right-click the graph and search for GetFollowCamera (no spaces) and select the Get Follow Camera node. This is the getter node for the Camera included with the character in Components. (Alternatively, you can drag the Follow Camera from the Components tab onto the graph to create the node).

From the output pin of this node, drag a wire, search for GetWorldLocation, and select it. This node shows the Camera component's location in the world space. Connect the GetWorldLocation yellow output to the Start input of Line trace node (see Figure 5-13).

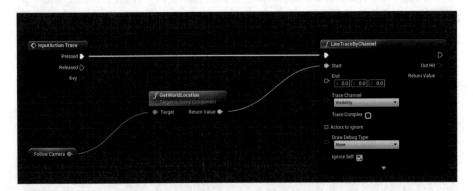

Figure 5-13. *Setting up line trace start location*

Now you need the trace to end at a specified length where the Camera is looking. To do that, drag a wire from Follow Camera, and search for and select GetWorldRotation, which represents the world rotation of the Camera Component. To find the direction, drag a wire from the GetWorldRotation blue output, and search for and select GetForwardVector.

The GetForwardVector node represents the direction, but it returns a unit vector, which means it is in the 0–1 range and is not useful in our context (https://en.wikipedia.org/wiki/Rotation_matrix). So you multiply it by a higher number to determine how far the trace should go.

Drag a wire from the GetForwardVector node's yellow output, search for **multiply** and select the vector * float node. After selecting this node, enter **5000** in the green box of the newly created multiply node. The 5000 is the length of our trace. Connect the multiply node output to the End input of the Line Trace node.

Next, click the Visibility drop-down button on the Line Trace node and change it to MyItemTrace (see Figure 5-14).

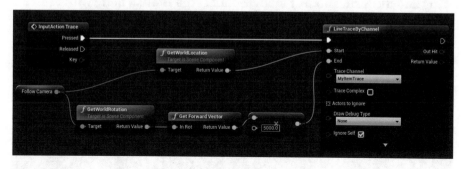

Figure 5-14. *Setting up line trace end location*

You are not completely done, but you did finish the trace setup. If you play the game now and press E (or the key you used for Trace), it might appear that nothing is happening, but you are tracing. To check this, click the None drop-down button at Draw Debug Type and change it to For Duration. Press the Play button again and start the tracing. You now see a red line originating from your Camera that shoots toward where you are looking.

Even though you finished the trace, you are still not using any information from the hit result. Let's fix that. Drag a pin from the red Return Value of the Line Trace, search, and select Branch node. The return value is a boolean (either true or false). It is true if the hit is successful (if it hits any object with MyItemTrace, trace response is blocking; in our case, it is the Blueprint actor we created). It is false if the trace didn't hit anything. Drag another wire from the Out Hit node and select Break Hit Result. The resulting node is called a Struct node, which is a container containing other data types.

In the Break Hit Result node, click the downward arrow to expand the node and show all the advanced types. Right-click the event graph, and search for and select Print String, which is a simple node that prints a message to the screen. Drag a wire from Hit Actor and connect it to In String of Print String. This automatically creates a new node between Print String and the Struct node. Finally, connect the Branch node with Print String, and you have a complete setup (see Figure 5-15).

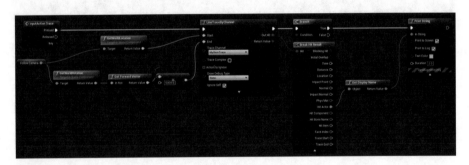

Figure 5-15. *Adding debug setup with Print Node*

Since you need the trace to react, you must place the Blueprint you created. Drag and drop the Blueprint from the Content Browser to the game world. Now press Play and look at the item placed in the world. Press your Trace input key. You see a red trace line (if you set the Draw Debug Type to For Duration or Persistent) hitting the item and a message printed on the screen (see Figure 5-16).

Figure 5-16. *Print node outputs correct information*

Destruction Using Physics

In this section, you use the Apex destruction plugin to create a destructible mesh and interact with it in the game. When writing this book, Unreal Engine was making the transition from Physx to Chaos Physics System, rendering this section obsolete in the future. I don't cover Chaos because it is not production-ready and requires the GitHub source version instead of the launcher version.

To create a destructible mesh, you first need to enable the Apex plugin from the Plugins section. Click the Edit button in the menu bar and select Plugins. Go to the Physics category and enable Apex Destruction Plugin. Restart the Editor (see Figure 5-17).

Figure 5-17. *Enabling Apex Destruction plugin*

After the restart, you can right-click any Static Mesh actor (or 1M_Cube in our case) in the Content Browser and select Create Destructible Mesh. A new Destructible Editor opens and a new Destructible Editor actor is available next to the static mesh. Let's go through the basics of Destructible Mesh Editor in Figure 5-18.

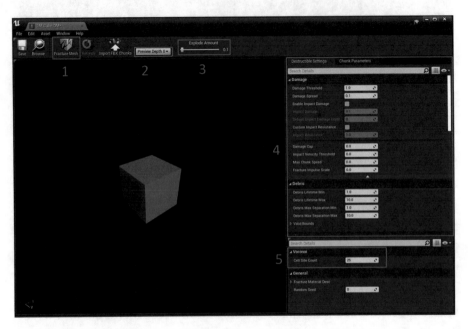

Figure 5-18. *Destructible Editor layout*

- **Fracture Mesh** (area 1 in Figure 5-18) fractures the mesh into multiple chunks. The number of chunks is based on the Cell Site Count under the Voronoi section (bottom-right corner).

- **Preview Depth 0** (area 2 in Figure 5-18) is the chunk depth.

- **Explode Amount** (area 3 in Figure 5-18) is a slider that moves the fractured pieces apart.

- **Destructible Settings** (area 4 in Figure 5-18) is the panel where you adjust various destructible settings.

- **Fracture settings** (area 5 in Figure 5-18) is the area where you decide the number of chunks to generate.

First, set the Cell Site Count to 100 and press the Fracture Mesh button. This breaks the mesh into 100 different chunk pieces (see Figure 5-19).

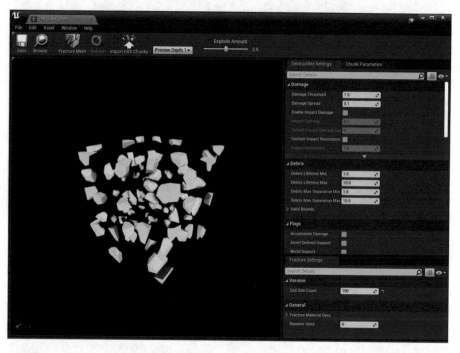

Figure 5-19. *100 pieces of mesh*

Go back to the Content Browser and drag the newly created Destructible Mesh actor (1M_Cube_DM) to the game world. If you press the Play button now, nothing happens because the destructible mesh is not simulating physics. To fix it, select the Destructible actor in the viewport, and in the Details panel, enable Simulate Physics (see Figure 5-20).

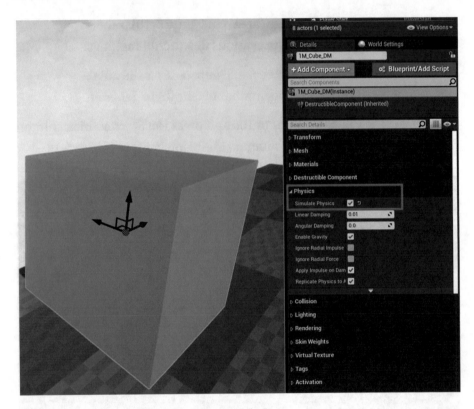

Figure 5-20. *Simulate Physics enabled*

Now, if you press Play, you see the destructible mesh falling and hitting the ground, but there is no destruction. Why? This is destructible mesh, but there is no destruction, right? Well, this is because you haven't enabled damage to destruction mesh yet. So how do you do that? Open the Destructible Mesh actor and turn on Enable Impact Damage (see Figure 5-21).

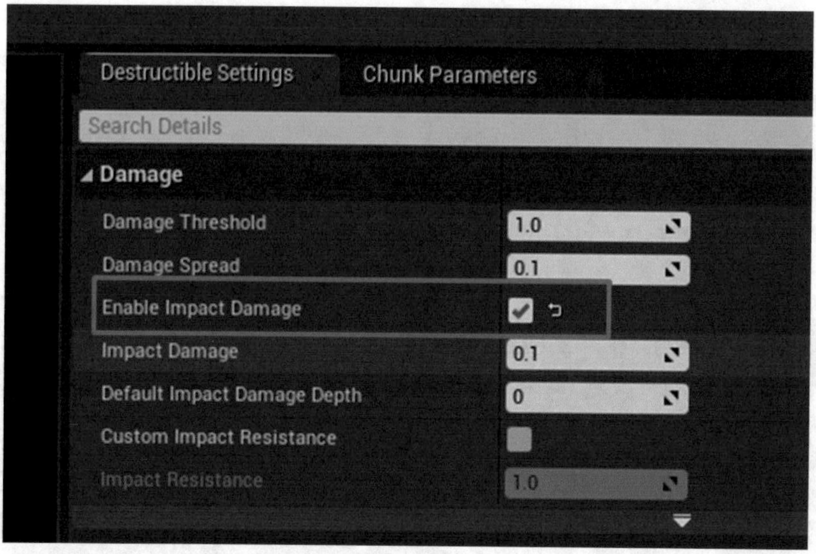

Figure 5-21. Impact Damage enabled

Go back to your game world and press Play. Watch how the mesh falls
and breaks into pieces (see Figure 5-22).

Figure 5-22. Broken mesh after falling

Let's spice this up a little bit by applying a particle effect when the mesh breaks. For the particle system, add the Starter Content pack if not added yet. To add starter content, click the Add New button in the Content Browser and select the first Add Feature or Content Pack. In the next dialog window, switch to the Content Packs tab, select Starter Content, and click **+Add to Project** (see Figure 5-23).

Figure 5-23. *Adding Starter Content to our project*

After the Starter Content is added, open the 1M_Cube_DM, and in the Destruction Settings Details panel under the Effects category, expand Fracture Settings. Here you see two numbers: 0 and 1. Expand 1 and assign P_Smoke (which is the particle from Starter Content) (see Figure 5-24).

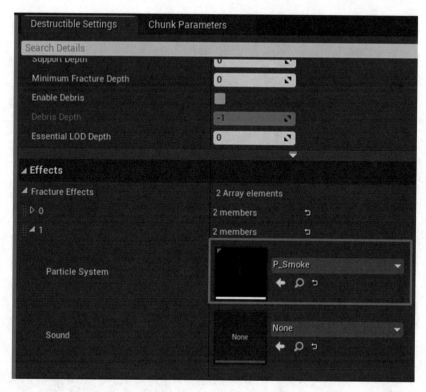

Figure 5-24. *Assigning smoke particle system*

If you play now, when the object falls and breaks, you see the particle effect playing at the fracture location (see Figure 5-25).

Figure 5-25. *Smoke effect being played after mesh breaks*

CHAPTER 6

Importing Meshes and Textures

Let's export the mesh from Autodesk 3ds Max and import it into Unreal Engine. First, open the 3ds Max scene with the mesh ready to export. Select Export from the File menu, and choose a location and name to save the FBX file. The FBX export options pop up to set the following settings because you are exporting a Static Mesh.

1. Expand the Geometry category and enable Smoothing Groups.

2. Expand the Animation, Cameras, and Lights categories and disable them.

3. (Optional) Disable Embed Media. You can include the textures inside the FBX file by enabling the Embed Media option.

4. Expand the Units category and enable Automatic conversion.

5. Finally, make sure the FBX file format is 2018, and then press OK. At the time of writing this book, the UE4 FBX import pipeline uses FBX 2018. Using an earlier or newer version might result in incompatibilities.

© Satheesh Pv 2021
S. Pv, *Beginning Unreal Engine 4 Blueprints Visual Scripting*,
https://doi.org/10.1007/978-1-4842-6396-9_6

After exporting the asset, open Unreal Engine and the Content Browser. Right-click inside an empty area and select the Import option. From the Import File Browser dialog, navigate to where you exported the asset, select it, and import. This opens the FBX Import Options dialog. Let's look at some of the important settings (see Figures 6-1a and 6-1b).

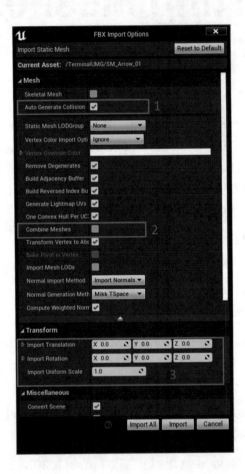

Figure 6-1a.

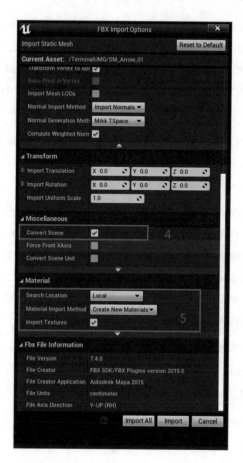

Figure 6-1b.

- **Auto Generate Collision** (area 1 in Figure 6-1a)
  automatically generates a collision for your mesh if no
  custom collision is included inside the FBX file.

- **Combine Meshes** (area 2 in Figure 6-1a) is an
  advanced option. If you have multiple meshes inside a
  single FBX file, enabling this option combines them in
  a single mesh.

- **Import Translation/Rotation and Scale** (area 3 in Figure 6-1a) adjusts the location, rotation, and scale of the imported mesh relative to the FBX file. That means if you input 2 in Uniform Scale, then the mesh is two times bigger than the original file.

- **Convert Scene** (area 4 in Figure 6-1b) converts the FBX coordinate system to UE4 coordinate system. It is recommended to leave this option on.

- **Import Textures** (area 5 in Figure 6-1b). Since we chose not to embed media while exporting the FBX file, this option does not do anything because there is no embedded media. If your mesh is textured and you choose to embed media while exporting, then enabling this option imports the associated textures as well.

Since this mesh is already textured, I imported all the associated textures and created a material to apply to the mesh. The following are some tips to remember when creating textures.

- Only the following formats are supported.

  - BMP

  - PNG

  - TGA

  - JPG

  - PSD: Photoshop file

  - PCX: PiCture eXchange

  - EXR or HDR: OpenEXR or HDR format typically used with environment maps

  - DDS: Cubemap Texture

- All textures (except for the user interface/HUD) must be a power of two (e.g., 32×32, 64×64, 128×128, 256×256, 128×32, 512×256, 2048×512, etc.) The maximum texture resolution supported by Unreal Engine is 8192, but the display in the game is limited to 4096.

- It is highly recommended to use Packed textures for grayscale textures whenever possible since the UE4 Material Editor can read individual channels from the texture. For example, set the Roughness texture to the Red channel, Metallic to the Green channel, Ambient Occlusion to the Blue channel, and Emissive to the Alpha channel. This kind of workflow is more efficient and reduces the number of textures from 4 to 1.

You need to know about each texture and how it is useful, including individual texture channels. First, let's look at some of the common texture terminologies because they are important.

- **Diffuse** (Non-PBR): This map defines the look of your object. Imagine taking a photograph in front of a brick wall to use as a diffuse map. It includes all the lighting information and shadow details.

- **Albedo** (PBR): The same as diffuse but without any lighting or shadow information.

- **Specular** (Non-PBR): Typically, a grayscale map that defines where the reflections should appear.

- **Roughness** (PBR): A grayscale map that defines the sharpness of reflections. Closer to white means it is rougher, so light scatters in more directions, making the reflection blurry. Closer to black means it is smoother and makes the reflection sharper.

Note   Some software might call this map Gloss. The terms *gloss* and *roughness* are interchangeable, and they are inverted to each other.

- **Metallic** (PBR): A black and white map that defines how metal-like your surface is. The reason you use either black or white is that surfaces are either metallic or non-metallic. Anything between 0 and 1 is a rare use case.

- **Normal** (PBR and Non-PBR): A purple color map representing different direction axes for each channel. It provides additional high-micro details to the surface.

- **Ambient Occlusion** (AO) (PBR and Non-PBR): A black and white map containing micro shadows or detailed shadows. Multiply this map with Albedo.

Some of the textures (also known as maps) have PBR and Non-PBR written next to them. This means that the map is only useful in that specific workflow. PBR stands for Physically Based Rendering, which is used by UE4 and all modern game engines.

Now that you have an idea of textures, let's import them to Unreal Engine. Navigate to the folder where you have the textures and either drag and drop directly to the Content Browser or right-click Content Browser and import it just like you did for our mesh.

Creating Material

To use textures, you need to create Materials, which define an object's look and feel. You can set how shiny a material is, how the texture should look, its transparency, and so on. Inside Material, you create expression nodes to define how the material feels. To create a Material, right-click inside the Content Browser and select Material. After that, double-click the newly created material to open the Material Editor. You see a Graph Editor, as shown in Figure 6-2.

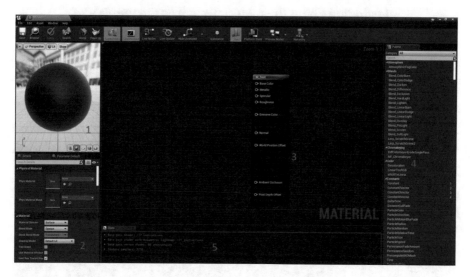

Figure 6-2.

The Material Editor is divided into four parts.

- **Viewport** (area 1 in Figure 6-2) is where you see the final material.

- The **Details panel** (area 2 in Figure 6-2) is where you edit the selected node's properties (also known as material expression node). If no nodes are selected, then the properties of the material are shown.

- **Graph Editor** (area 3 in Figure 6-2) is where you create your material expression nodes network. By default, it starts with a single base node with a series of input that you can connect to material expressions.

107

- The **Palette panel** (area 4 in Figure 6-2) contains a list of all nodes that can be dragged and dropped into the Graph Editor.

- The **Stats panel** (area 5 in Figure 6-2) shows important information about the material, such as the number of instructions and the number of texture samples.

Let's apply basic color to our material. Press and hold the 3 key on your keyboard. Left-click your mouse inside the Graph Editor to create a vector3 node. Or right-click inside the Graph Editor, search for Constant3Vector and select that node. Once created, right-click the selected node and select Convert to Parameter. You are prompted to enter a name for the new node. To keep things simple, let's call it **Color** and connect the first white color pin to the Base Color node of your material. The resulting graph should look like Figure 6-3.

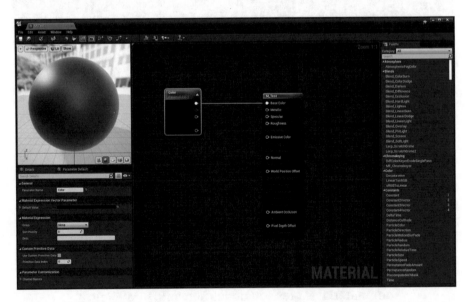

Figure 6-3.

The parameter value you created can modify at runtime via C++ or Blueprints.

Material Types

Before you continue with the material, let's look at the different types of materials available in Unreal Engine. Materials are of three types.

- **Material**: The main material that you just created.

- **Material Instance Constant**: An instanced material (basically a child of main material) cannot change its properties at runtime.

- **Material Instance Dynamic**: An instanced material that can change its properties runtime. It can only be created at runtime via Blueprints or C++ and cannot be accessed through the Content Browser.

Material Instances (both Constant and Dynamic) are used to change the appearance of material without recompiling the main material. Any change you make in the main Material Editor always requires a recompiling of shaders, which takes time if it is very complicated material. To save time, you can choose to parameterize certain nodes from the main material to be changed without recompiling the material. This is what you did by creating a Constant3Vector node and converting it to a parameter.

Go back to THE Content Browser, right-click the material you just added, and select Create Material Instance from the context menu (see Figure 6-4).

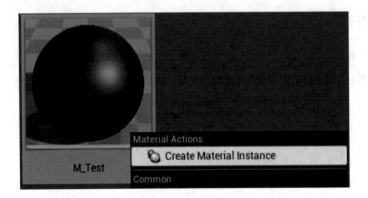

Figure 6-4.

You now have a new asset right next to the Material, which is our Instanced Material. Open it, and you should see a window similar to the screenshot shown in Figure 6-5.

Figure 6-5.

- The **viewport** (area 1 in Figure 6-5) is where you see the Material Instance changes.

- The **Details panel** (area 2 in Figure 6-5) lists all the parameters from the parent material. Here you can override or change them and see the changes immediately on the viewport. By default, parameters are not overridden; to override them, left-click the grayed-out checkbox next to the parameter name.

Let's change the color of this material instance to something blueish. To do so, override the color parameter and click the default color to open the color picker. Feel free to select any color you like (see Figure 6-6).

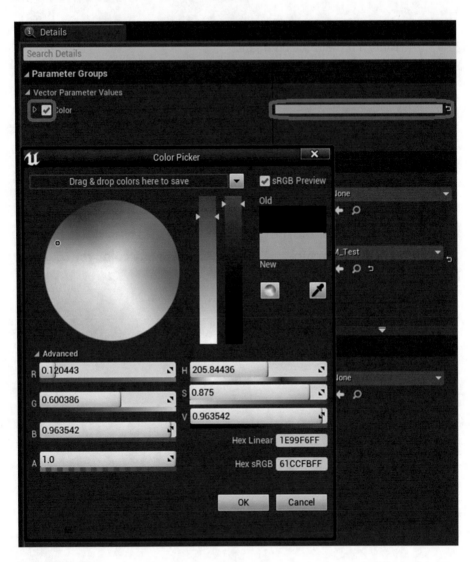

Figure 6-6.

As you change the color, the viewport updates the changes in real time without delay.

Go back to the Content Browser, open the original material you created before, change the color, and apply. You see that the viewport temporarily changes the material to a grid-based material before showing that you the changed color. This is because of shader recompiling.

In addition to all the material types mentioned, two other types are helpful with material workflow.

- Material Functions

- Material Parameter Collection

Material Functions are essentially a collection of different material expression nodes that you can reuse in materials. Think of them as a container, or package, or group of nodes with input and output. If you often create a series of nodes, and you find yourself reusing them, then its best you create a material function and keep those series of nodes inside a function graph.

Unreal Engine 4 already includes several material functions that commonly use shader operations such as blending, fuzzy shading, simple grass wind, and more. They can take any input and do the processing based on input and other parameters, and send output.

Material Parameter Collection is a data asset that stores a set of scalar and vector parameters used in any material. This collection can be accessed from anywhere, making it a powerful tool to send global data to multiple materials.

Material Functions Example

To demonstrate a material function, let's create a simple one that pans the texture in X and Y directions. To create a material function, click the Content Browser, and under the Materials & Textures category, select Material Function (see Figure 6-7).

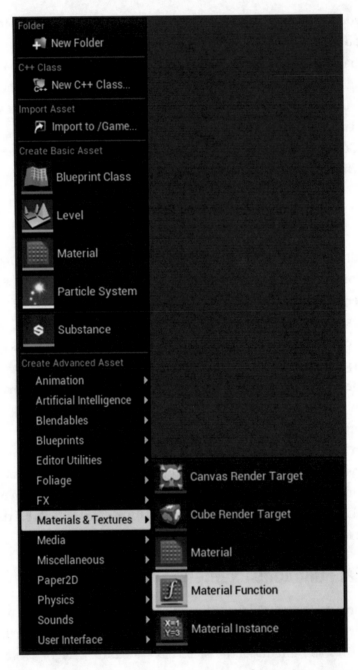

Figure 6-7.

After it's created, give it a name (e.g., MyMaterialFunction) and double-click to open it. Once you open, you see a default output (which should be selected by default) node, and the material should be saying Missing function output result. This is because a material function can have multiple inputs and outputs. You can preview the output by right-clicking the output node and selecting Start Previewing. By default, Unreal Engine previews the default output node, and since no nodes are connected, it simply reports the error. To fix it for now, right-click the blue output node and select Stop Previewing Node (see Figure 6-8). This removes the error.

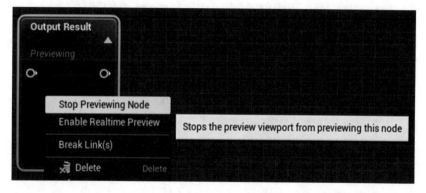

Figure 6-8.

You created a material function for panning texture, so let's get started.

1. Press and hold the T key on your keyboard, and left-click inside the graph or right-click inside the graph, and search for Texture Sample and select it.

2. Right-click inside the graph and search for Function Input and select it. These nodes serve as a way to pass data into the graph (similar to function inputs in programming languages). Since you want the ability to use any texture, you use it as an input.

3. In the Details panel (make sure the input node is selected), set the Function Input to Function Input Texture 2D and set Input Name to Texture (this can be any name you like, as it serves no purpose other than being visible outside the graph). Connect this node to the Texture Input of the previously created Texture Sample node.

4. Right-click inside the graph and search for Texture Object and select it. You use this node to feed a default value for the Input node previously created. Connect the Texture node to the Preview input of the function input node.

5. Right-click the graph, search for Panner, and select it. This is the main node that does the panning or moving. Connect the panner output to the UVs pin of the Texture Sample node.

6. Create another function input node and select it. Set the Function Input to Function Input Vector 2 and connect it to the Speed input of the previously created Panner node. Make sure Use Preview Value as Default is enabled.

7. Right-click the graph, search for Constant2Vector node, and select it. Set the default value to 0.1 on both R and G for the Constant2Vector and connect it to the Preview input of the function node previously created.

8. The only thing left is to connect the Texture Sample node's output to the main output node. Right-click the final output node and select Start Previewing Node.

You should now have a graph similar to Figure 6-9.

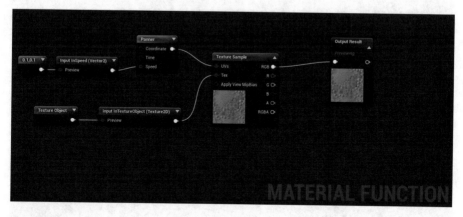

Figure 6-9.

To expose it to materials, make sure you have no nodes selected. In the Details panel, enable Expose to Library. Expand the Libraries Category Text section. Replace the Misc category to any name you like and save the material function. For example, I changed it to Apress Book (see Figure 6-10).

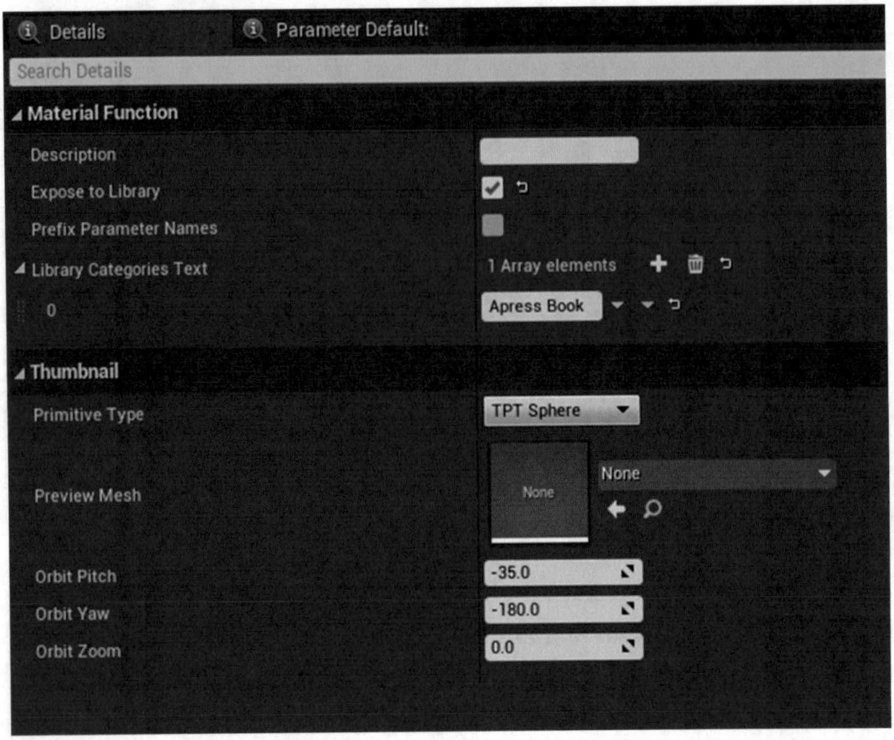

Figure 6-10.

Going back to the main material created at the beginning of this chapter, right-click inside the graph. You should see the new material function ready to be used (see Figure 6-11).

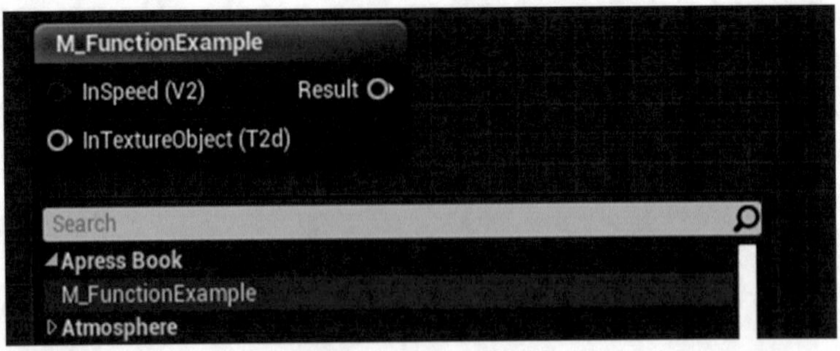

Figure 6-11.

Modifying Materials at Runtime Using Blueprint and C++

In the Material Types section, I mentioned that material properties can be changed using the Material Instance Dynamic. This section looks at how to create a material instance dynamic using the material you created and change its color at runtime.

Using Blueprints

For this material runtime chapter, you use a static mesh that comes with Unreal Engine so you can easily follow along.

Open or go to Content Browser, right-click in an empty area, and select Blueprint Class. Select Actor as our base from the Pick Parent Class dialog and give it a name (e.g., BP_MyActor). Double-click the newly created Blueprint class to open it. After opening, you see the Viewport tab in the middle and the Components tab on the right side.

Click the green + Add Component button and select Static Mesh from the list. You can rename it to anything you like, and for this example, I renamed it MyStaticMeshComponent. Select the newly created Static Mesh Component, and from the Details panel under the Static Mesh category, click the drop-down button labeled None. This opens a drop-down in which you can select the mesh you want to assign. Since you use a mesh that comes with the engine, click the View Options button and select Show Engine Content (see Figure 6-12).

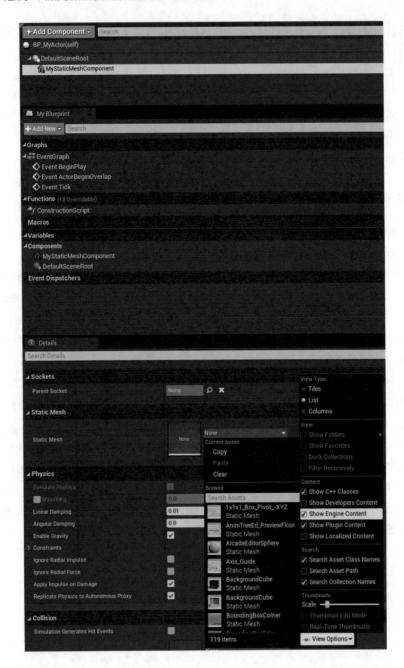

Figure 6-12.

Next, search for SM_MatPreview and select SM_MatPreviewMesh_01. You should see the new mesh in the Viewport tab. Now that you assigned our required mesh, you no longer require to show Engine Content. Go to the same View Options and uncheck Show Engine Content.

You are now done with assigning the mesh, but you still need to change the material at runtime. The following explains how to do it.

1. Switch to the Construction Script tab, right-click inside the graph, and search for Create Dynamic Material Instance. Select the first node.

2. In the newly created node, click the parent button (where it says Select Asset) and select the previously created material. It doesn't matter whether you select the main parent material or one of its instances.

3. Since you change this at runtime, you need a reference to this dynamic material instance. Click, drag, and release from the Return Value pin and select Promote To Variable. Let's call this new variable MID (short form for Material Instance Dynamic).

4. Click the MyStaticMeshComponent from the Components tab and drag it to the graph. This automatically creates a getter node for MyStaticMeshComponent. From the output pin of MyStaticMeshComponent, left-click and drag a new wire and release it. From the resulting context menu, search for Set Material and select it. Make sure you select Set Material and not Set Material by Name.

5. Connect Set MID node to Set Material node.

6. Right-click the graph again, search for Get MID, and select it. This is the same variable you created in step 3. Connect the MID node to the Material input of Set Material node created in step 4.

Figure 6-13 shows the completed graph.

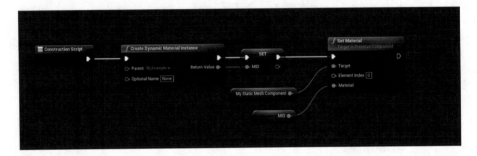

Figure 6-13.

Switch over to the Viewport tab, and you see the mesh is now colored black, which was the default color you assigned in Material (see Figure 6-14).

Figure 6-14.

Now it's time to create a new function to change the color dynamically.
Switch back to the Construction Script tab and create the Get MID node
again. Drag a wire from the MID node and select the Set Vector Parameter
Value node. In this node, set Parameter Name to Color, which was the
same name you set in the Material Editor (see Figure 6-15).

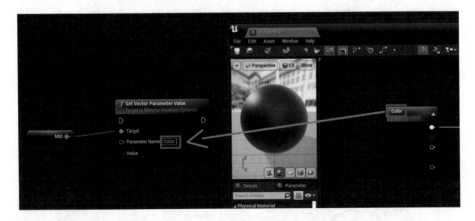

Figure 6-15.

You create a function node to easily switch the colors. To create a function, take the following steps.

1. Select both the MID node and the Set Vector Parameter Value node. (Press **Ctrl** and select them.)

2. Right-click any one of the selected nodes.

3. Select **Collapse to Function** (see Figure 6-16).

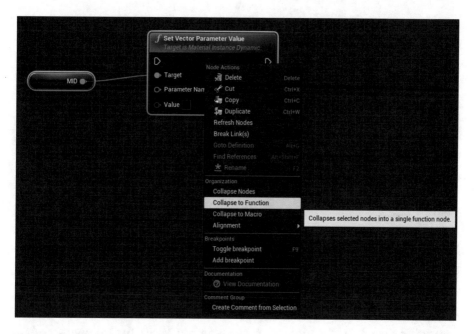

Figure 6-16.

In the My Blueprints tab, you are prompted to rename this new function, so let's call it ChangeColorTo. Double-click this new node to open the graph and drag the Value pin of Set Vector Parameter Value on to the purple Change Color To node. You should see the Add Pin to Node tooltip (see Figure 6-17).

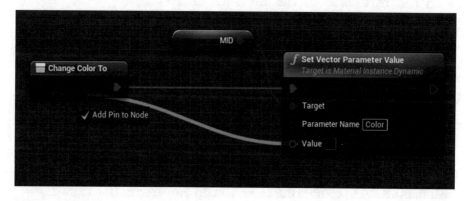

Figure 6-17.

Release the left mouse button when you see this tooltip, and you now have a Value input for this function connected to the Set Vector Parameter Value node.

Go back to Construction Script and connect the newly created Change Color To node after Set Material node. For the value, set a different color (e.g., red) and compile. Switch back to the Viewport tab, and you see the red color applied. You now have a function that can be called anytime during gameplay to change the color.

Using C++

Now that you know how to use Blueprints to make changes to runtime material, let's dig into C++ and see how things are done. In Chapter 4, you already made an Actor class that you can modify. The first thing you need to do is expose a variable with the type Material to Blueprints, so you have a material to create Material Instance Dynamic. Write the following code in the MyActor.h header file.

```
/* Material to be used as the parent for Material Instance
Dynamic. */
UPROPERTY(EditAnywhere)
class UMaterialInterface* ParentMaterial;

/* Cached reference to the instance created. */
UPROPERTY()
class UMaterialInstanceDynamic* MID;

/* Use this color in MID. */
UPROPERTY(EditAnywhere)
FLinearColor NewColor;
```

In Blueprints, you might have noticed that you created the dynamic material instance inside Construction Script, and you created a custom function to change the color. You do the same in C++ using the

OnConstruction native method and a custom function. In MyActor.h
header file, add the following code.

```
/* This is the same as Construction Script in Blueprints */
virtual void OnConstruction(const FTransform& Transform) override;
```

```
/* You create the same function from Blueprint, which can
change the color in MID. */
UFUNCTION(BlueprintCallable, Category = "My Actor")
void ChangeColorTo();
```

Now to implement, add the following code to the MyActor.cpp file.

```
void AMyActor::OnConstruction(const FTransform& Transform)
{
    Super::OnConstruction(Transform);

    // Make sure you have a valid material to create from.
    if (ParentMaterial != nullptr)
    {
        // Create the dynamic material instance using the
        static Create method.
        MID = UMaterialInstanceDynamic::Create(ParentMateri
        al, this);

// Assign the material to Mesh Component.
MeshComponent->SetMaterial(0, MID);

    }
}

void AMyActor::ChangeColorTo()
{
    // It is important to check if MID is valid.
    if (MID != nullptr)
    {
```

```
        // Set the color to NewColor value.
        MID->SetVectorParameterValue(FName("Color"), NewColor);
    }
}
```

It is possible to directly reference assets from the Content Browser in C++. You take a quick look at assigning the parent material directly in C++.

First, right-click the material from Content Browser and select Copy Reference, which copies the clipboard's reference path. You use this path with a slight modification in C++ (see Figure 6-18).

Figure 6-18.

Open MyActor.cpp file and under the AMyActor constructor and add the following code.

```
static ConstructorHelpers::FObjectFinder<UMaterialInterface>
ContentBrowserMaterial(TEXT(""));
```

Now inside the quotation marks of (TEXT("")), paste the reference path that you copied from content browser from the clipboard. It should now look like this (Note: Path might differ based on where the material is)

```
static ConstructorHelpers::FObjectFinder<UMaterialInterface>
ContentBrowserMaterial(TEXT("Material'/Game/Blueprints/M_
Example.M_Example'"));.
```

Next, add this condition flow beneath the last line.

```
if (ContentBrowserMaterial.Succeeded())
{
    ParentMaterial = ContentBrowserMaterial.Object;
}
```

Your constructor code should now look like the following.

```
AMyActor::AMyActor()
{
    MeshComponent = CreateDefaultSubobject<UStaticMeshComponent>
    (TEXT("MeshComponent"));
    RootComponent = MeshComponent;

    bCanBeCollected = true;
    ToggleableOption = 0;
    static ConstructorHelpers::FObjectFinder<UMaterialInt
    erface> ContentBrowserMaterial(TEXT("Material'/Game/
    Blueprints/M_Example.M_Example'"));
    if (ContentBrowserMaterial.Succeeded())
    {
        ParentMaterial = ContentBrowserMaterial.Object;
    }
    PrimaryActorTick.bCanEverTick = true;
}
```

Run the game by pressing F5 in Visual Studio. Once the Editor has started, open the Blueprint based on MyActor, which you created in Chapter 4. You should now see the new Parent Material and New Color in Blueprint Editor. Drag and drop the Blueprint to the game viewport. You now see the mesh is colored black, which is the default color (see Figure 6-19).

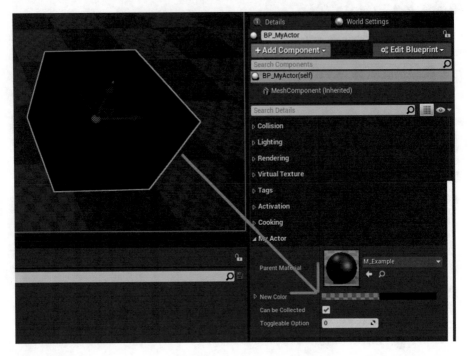

Figure 6-19.

You can adjust the new color to any other color and see the change immediately. Since you also exposed Change Color To function in C++ to Blueprint, you can call it anytime during gameplay.

CHAPTER 7

Demo Game

In this final chapter, you create a demo game using the default First Person Shooter Template (Blueprint version) that comes with Unreal Engine (Launcher version) and extend it to include various features, such as ammo count, ammo pickup, and so forth. After the features are done, you learn how to package the game for Windows.

Creating the Project

Let's start by creating a project using the First Person Template. Open Epic Games Launcher and click the big yellow Launch button in the top-right corner. This starts Unreal Engine, and soon, you are greeted with the Unreal Project Browser window (see Figure 7-1).

© Satheesh Pv 2021
S. Pv, *Beginning Unreal Engine 4 Blueprints Visual Scripting*,
https://doi.org/10.1007/978-1-4842-6396-9_7

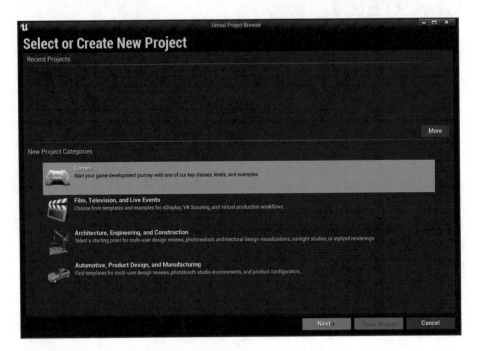

Figure 7-1 *.Unreal Project Browser*

Select Games and click Next. From the template selection screen, select the First Person template and click Next (see Figure 7-2).

Figure 7-2. *Select First Person Template*

In the Project Settings page, you set the initial settings for your project and the type (Blueprint or C++). Start with a C++ project and create Blueprints. Choose C++, set a location, name your project, and click Create Project. It's important to remember that the files are named in this context: <ProjectName><ClassType>.h. In this example, I named the project Chapter07, so my files are named based on that—for example, Chapter07Character, Chapter07GameMode and so on (see Figure 7-3).

Figure 7-3. *Choose C++ project type*

Once the project is created, Visual Studio automatically opens with the project's solution file. Unreal Editor also starts. Press the Play button (or **Alt+P**) on the toolbar to test the FPS template. While playing, use the W key to move forward, S to move back, A to strafe left, D to strafe right, the mouse to look around, and left mouse button to shoot projectiles. The template also includes basic physics simulation, so that when you shoot any of the white boxes, it tumbles around (see Figure 7-4).

Figure 7-4. *Physics enabled boxes*

Ammo Setup

As you may have noticed, you can shoot the projectiles as much as you want. We need to change this. We need settings for the number of clips the weapon can have and the amount of ammo per clip. For example, if this weapon has 3 clips and 20 rounds of ammo per clip, then the maximum amount of ammo this weapon can have is 3 * 20 = 60. Every time you shoot 20 rounds of ammo, each clip is depleted. There is a two-second timeout before shooting the next clip. In a real project, this timeout is replaced by a reload animation. We will use variables to define the values so you can adjust everything without having to worry about the inner workings.

To have ammo functionality, open the Chapter07Character.h Header file. The following variables are created under GENERATED_BODY() macro.

- **Max Clips** (integer): The maximum number of clips the weapon can have. Default 5.

- **Starting Clips** (integer): The number of clips the weapon has when the game starts. This should never be greater than Max Clips. Default 3.

- **Ammo Per Clip** (integer): The amount of ammo per clip. Default 20.

- **Current Clips** (integer): The number of clips the weapon currently has. Every time the weapon reloads, subtract this variable by one to denote that the clip has been used. Default 0.

- **Current Ammo** (integer): The amount of ammo the weapon currently has. Every time you shoot, subtract this variable by one to denote that you fired one bullet. Default 0.

- **bCanShoot** (boolean): True or false variable that determines if you can shoot or not. Default false.

- **ReloadTime**: Time in seconds for the weapon to reload when all bullets have fired. Default 2.

Since you want them to be exposed to the Editor, mark them as UPROPERTY. The following is the code for the variables. Note the usage of BlueprintReadOnly and BlueprintReadWrite.

```
/* Maximum amount of clips this weapon is allowed to have.  */
    UPROPERTY(EditDefaultsOnly, BlueprintReadOnly)
    int32 MaxClips;
```

```
/* Amount of clips for the weapon to have when the game
starts. This should never be greater than Max Clips. */
UPROPERTY(EditDefaultsOnly, BlueprintReadWrite)
int32 StartingClips;
  /* Amount of ammo per clip. */
UPROPERTY(EditDefaultsOnly, BlueprintReadOnly)
int32 AmmoPerClip;
/* True or false variable that determines if you can shoot
or not. */
UPROPERTY(EditDefaultsOnly, BlueprintReadWrite)
bool bCanShoot;
/* Time in seconds for the weapon to reload when all
bullets are fired. */
UPROPERTY(EditDefaultsOnly, BlueprintReadOnly)
float ReloadTime;
/* Amount of clips this weapon currently has. Every time
the weapon reloads, you subtract this variable by one to
denote that the clip has been used. */
UPROPERTY(BlueprintReadWrite)
int32 CurrentClips;
/* Amount of ammo this weapon currently has. Every time
you shoot, you subtract this variable by one to denote
that you fired one bullet. */
UPROPERTY(BlueprintReadWrite)
int32 CurrentAmmo;
```

After setting up the variables, let's create our initial logic in the Construction Script graph. Before that, you must assign default values to these variables; otherwise, they are 0 and false. Open Chapter07Character.cpp. At the top of the file (around line 20), you see the AChapter07Character constructor (e.g., AChapter07Character::AChapter07Character()). Inside this block, assign the default variables as follows.

```
MaxClips = 5;
StartingClips = 3;
AmmoPerClip = 20;
CurrentClips = 0;
CurrentAmmo = 0;
bCanShoot = false;
ReloadTime = 2.f;
```

Press F5 to compile and start the project from Visual Studio. After the Editor has started, open FirstPersonCharacter Blueprint and the Construction Script graph.

Drag a wire from Construction Script's output pin, search for Sequence node, and add it. The Sequence node is a special Blueprint node that allows you to run multiple outputs (you can add as many outputs as you want) from top to bottom. Add a Branch node and connect the first output of the Sequence node (with the label Then 0) to the Branch node.

You need to use the Branch node condition to ensure that Starting Clips is not greater than Max Clips. Drag and drop both Starting Clips and Max Clips from the My Blueprints tab to the Construction Script graph. Drag a pin from Starting Clips, search for the > symbol, and select integer > integer node (Starting Clips is now automatically connected to the first input of the > node). This node returns true if the first input is greater than the second input, so connect Max Clips to the second input of > (greater than) node and connect the red output to the Condition input of the Branch node.

To set the value for the Starting Clip node, press and hold the Alt key on your keyboard, and then drag and drop the Starting Clip node again from the Blueprints tab to the Construction Script graph. This creates the Set node for Starting Clips. Connect the True output of the Branch node to the Set node. Connect Max Clips as the new input for the Set Starting Clip node. The graph should like Figure 7-5.

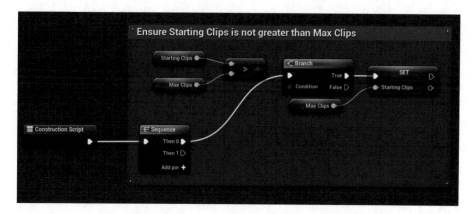

Figure 7-5. *Ammo setup. Setting starting clips*

The second step is to set the current ammo for this weapon. You need to set current ammo only if you have at least one clip to start with. So you first set Current Clips to Starting Clips and then check if Current Clips is greater than 0. If it is, then you set the Current Ammo to the same value as Ammo Per Clip. If Current Clips is 0, then Current Ammo is also 0. The second step of the graph should look like Figure 7-6.

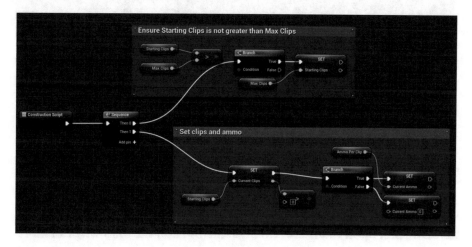

Figure 7-6. *Ammo setup. Setting current ammo*

The last step in the Construction Graph is to determine if you can shoot or not. Create the following nodes.

1. Set node for the Can Shoot boolean variable.

2. Get the node for Current Ammo.

3. Greater than integer node (Integer > integer).

Connect the Current Ammo node to the first input of the > node, and connect the red output of the > node to the Set Can Shoot node. The final graph should look like Figure 7-7.

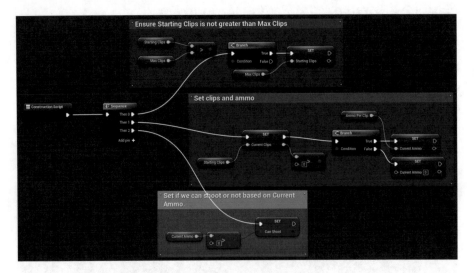

Figure 7-7. *Setting if we can shoot*

You have now defined a basic logic for ammo and clips, so it's time to make use of them.

Since this is done in Blueprint, let's make a function that is called on Blueprint Graph whenever the player shoots a bullet. To create the function, first open Chapter07Character.h and add the following function.

```
/* Event called whenever the player shoots. */
UFUNCTION(BlueprintImplementableEvent, Category = "Chapter 07
Character")
void OnFireEvent();
```

Then open Chapter07Character.cpp and find the OnFire() function (it should be around line 140). Inside this function, add a new if condition that will only proceed if bCanShoot is true. Then inside the if condition at the end, call our OnFireEvent Blueprint Event that was added before. The following is the full code for the modified OnFire function.

```
void AChapter07Character::OnFire()
{
    // See if you can shoot first.
    if (bCanShoot)
    {
        // try and fire a projectile
        if (ProjectileClass != NULL)
        {
            UWorld* const World = GetWorld();
            if (World != NULL)
            {
                if (bUsingMotionControllers)
                {
                    const FRotator SpawnRotation
                    = VR_MuzzleLocation-
                    >GetComponentRotation();
                    const FVector SpawnLocation
                    = VR_MuzzleLocation-
                    >GetComponentLocation();
                    World->SpawnActor<AChapter07
                    Projectile>(ProjectileClass,
                    SpawnLocation, SpawnRotation);
```

```
            }
            Else
            {
                    const FRotator SpawnRotation =
                    GetControlRotation();
                    // MuzzleOffset is in camera space,
                    so transform it to world space before
                    offsetting from the character location
                    to find the final muzzle position
                    const FVector SpawnLocation =
                    ((FP_MuzzleLocation != nullptr) ?
                    FP_MuzzleLocation->GetComponentLocation()
                    : GetActorLocation()) + SpawnRotation.
                    RotateVector(GunOffset);
                    //Set Spawn Collision Handling Override
                    FActorSpawnParameters ActorSpawnParams;
                    ActorSpawnParams.SpawnCollisionHandling
                    Override = ESpawnActorCollisionHandling
                    Method::AdjustIfPossibleButDontSpawnIf
                    Colliding;
                    // spawn the projectile at the muzzle
                    World->SpawnActor<AChapter07
                    Projectile>(ProjectileClass,
                    SpawnLocation, SpawnRotation,
                    ActorSpawnParams);
            }
        }
    }
    // try and play the sound if specified
    if (FireSound != NULL)
    {
```

```
        UGameplayStatics::PlaySoundAtLocation(this,
        FireSound, GetActorLocation());
    }
    // try and play a firing animation if specified
    if (FireAnimation != NULL)
    {
        // Get the animation object for the arms mesh
        UAnimInstance* AnimInstance = Mesh1P-
        >GetAnimInstance();
        if (AnimInstance != NULL)
        {
            AnimInstance->Montage_Play(FireAnimation,
            1.f);
        }
    }
    // Call the Blueprint event.
    OnFireEvent();
    }
}
```

Press F5 to compile and start the project from Visual Studio. Once the editor is started, open our FirstPersonCharacter Blueprint. Inside the Event Graph, right-click and search for On Fire Event. You can see the event that you declared in C++ is now accessible inside the Blueprint Graph (see Figure 7-8).

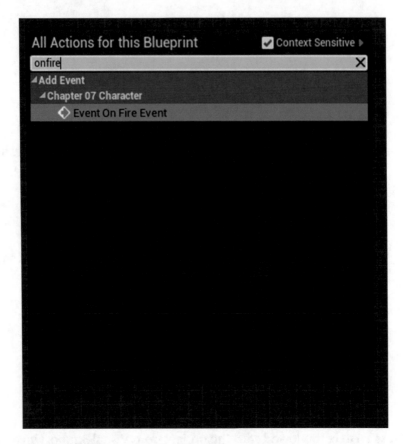

Figure 7-8. Add C++ event in Blueprint

Select it and right-click again in the graph, search for Get Current Ammo and select it. Drag a wire from the Current Ammo and search for Decrement Int and select it. This macro node takes an integer, subtracts it by 1, sets the value, and returns it, so the output pin contains the result of Current Ammo – 1.

If the output node of Decrement Int is not 0, don't do anything because the player can fire again. If it is 0, it means you ran out of ammo. To compare the results, right-click the graph, search for Compare Int, and add it. Then connect the Decrement Int node's output to the first input (with label Input) of Compare Int.

This is also a macro that has three output nodes and two input nodes. The first input node is the value to compare, and the second input is the value to compare with. If the first input value is greater than the second input, the first output triggers. If the first input is the same as the second input, then the second output is triggered. If the first input is less than the second input, the third output is triggered.

In our case, you are interested in the second output (with label ==) so set the input named Compare With to 0. Right-click the graph and search for Set Can Shoot. Add it to the graph and set it to false. Connect the second output of Compare Int (with label ==) to Set Can Shoot node. If the player tries to shoot now, nothing happens because you just told the weapon that it can't shoot once the current ammo is 0 (see Figure 7-9).

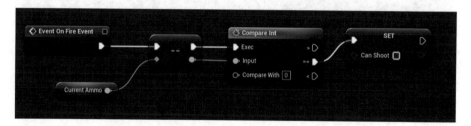

Figure 7-9. *Updating Current Ammo and Can Shoot variables*

This is where you add the reload logic. Right-click the graph, search for Set Timer By Event, and select it. This node can trigger a given event after a set time, which is the reload time. The event is the reload event. Right-click the graph, search for Get Reload Time and select it. Connect it to the Time input of the Set Timer node. Then drag a wire from the red input of Event input of the Set Timer node and select Custom Event from the Add Event section (see Figure 7-10).

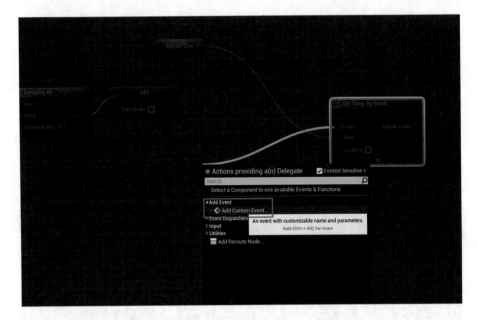

Figure 7-10. *Adding event to Timer*

After the event is selected, rename it Reload (or any name you like)
and connect the Can Shoot variable to the Set Timer By Event node (see
Figure 7-11).

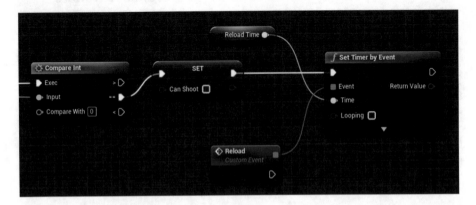

Figure 7-11. *Rename event to reload*

The Reload event is simple. In a nutshell, it is what is going to happen.

1. Check if you have any clips left. If you have a clip,
    then decrement it by one and set Current Ammo to
    Ammo per clip.

2. Enable or disable the Can Shoot variable based on
    Current Ammo (see Figure 7-12).

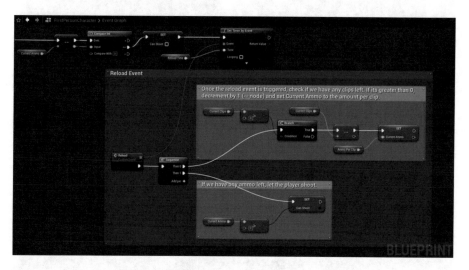

Figure 7-12. *Updating Can Shoot variable*

With the reload event done, you have finished our ammo setup. If
you go back to viewport, press play, and start firing, you eventually run
out of ammo, and it automatically reloads after 2 seconds. Once you run
completely out of clips, you won't be able to shoot the gun anymore.

From here, you move forward to implement a HUD and a pickup item.
First, you create a basic HUD using Unreal Motion Graphics (UMG), which
displays the amount of ammo you have. Then you move on to create an
ammo pickup item that replenishes ammo.

Head over to the Content Browser, right-click and select Widget
Blueprint from the User Interface category. You are prompted to rename
the Blueprint. Let's call it WBP_PlayerHUD (WBP is a short form of Widget
BluePrint). Open it, and add a text block from the Common category in the
bottom-right corner of the designer (see Figure 7-13).

147

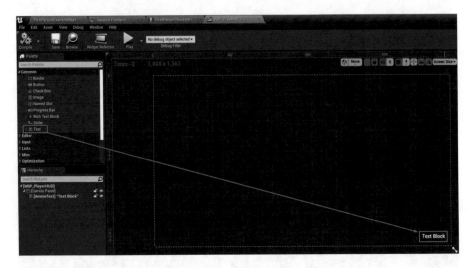

Figure 7-13. *Adding Text Block in UMG Designer*

Keep the text block selected. In the Details panel, set the name to AmmoText (or anything you want) and make sure Is Variable is selected (see Figure 7-14).

Figure 7-14. *Setting Ammo Text as variable*

It is important to set Is Variable to true; otherwise, you can't access it in the Event Graph. You can also expand the Anchors section and set Minimum and Maximum to 1. Now you can switch to the Graph tab (top-right corner) and create a new custom event by right-clicking inside the graph and selecting **Add Custom Event...** under the Add Event category. You call this new event UpdateAmmo and add two integer parameters. The first input is called CurrentAmmo, and the second input is called TotalAmmo. Since you enable Is Variable for AmmoText in the Designer tab, you can now drag and drop a reference to our text block from the My Blueprint tab. Drag a wire from the Ammo Text node and search for set text and select it. This node takes a Text input, so you create a formatted text using a special node. Right-click inside the graph, search for Format Text, and select that node. This node helps to build formatted text using curly braces {}.

Inside the Format input of the Format Text node, type **{Current}/ {Total}** and press Enter. The node now updates itself with two new gray input (a.k.a. wildcard) called Current and Total, which can directly accept any node (see Figure 7-15).

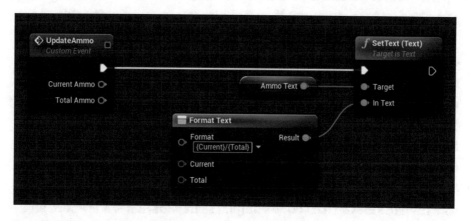

Figure 7-15. *Setting Text using Format Text node*

Connect the current ammo of the UpdateAmmo event to the Current gray input and connect the Total Ammo of UpdateAmmo event to the Total gray input (see Figure 7-16).

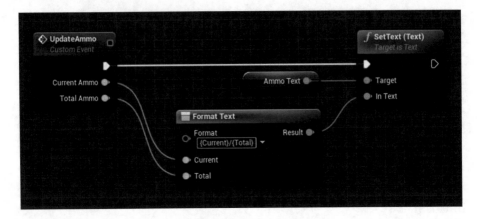

Figure 7-16. *After connecting to Format Text*

Now all that is left is to call this event from our First Person Character Blueprint class. To do that, you first need to create this HUD in that class. Open the FirstPersonCharacter Blueprint class and find the Event BeginPlay node. This node is automatically called when the game starts for this actor.

If you are not using VR (virtual reality), feel free to delete all the nodes connected to Event BeginPlay (for this tutorial, I'll delete them since VR is not our focus). Right-click the graph, search for Create Widget, and select that node. This node creates a widget based on the class input, so click the Select class button (purple input) and select our previously created WBP_PlayerHUD class. Right-click the Return Value output of Create Widget node and select Promote to Variable. This is because you want to access this later when ammo is changed. To add this widget to the screen, drag a wire from the PlayerHUD node's output, search for Add to Viewport, and select it (see Figure 7-17).

Figure 7-17. *Add Player HUD to viewport*

If you press Play (Alt+P) now, you can see the default text block (the one created in UMG designer) on the screen (see Figure 7-18).

Figure 7-18. *Game screen with Player HUD added*

Since you have to update the ammo whenever the game starts, you need to call the Update Ammo event in multiple places when you shoot and after reload. It's better to create a function, so from the My Blueprint tab, create a new function and name it UpdateAmmo. Open this function graph, and drag and drop the PlayerHUD (select Get PlayerHUD in the context menu) variable into this graph. Drag a wire from the PlayerHUD variable and search for Update Ammo and select it. You made two inputs for that, so for the first input, connect the Current Ammo variable. For the second input, you need the total ammo.

Remember, at the beginning of this chapter, I showed you how to get total ammo count using the number of clips and Ammo per Clip. To get the total ammo, first drag and drop Current Clips into the graph. From this Current Clips node, drag a wire, search for multiply node, and select integer

151

* integer. Now drag and drop Ammo Per Clip into the graph and connect it as the second input to the multiply node, and connect the multiply node to the second input of Update Ammo node (see Figure 7-19).

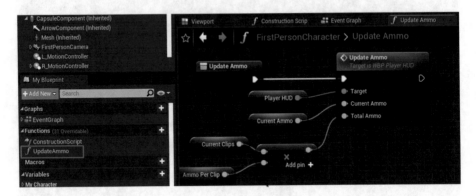

Figure 7-19. *Updating Ammo in Player HUD*

Now the only thing that remains is to call the function. You can drag and drop the function from the My Blueprints tab to the Event Graph. The first location where you call this function is at the end of the Begin Play execution chain (see Figure 7-20).

Figure 7-20. *Calling Update Ammo function after Begin Play*

The second location is right after reducing the Current Ammo count in the InputAction Fire node (see Figure 7-21).

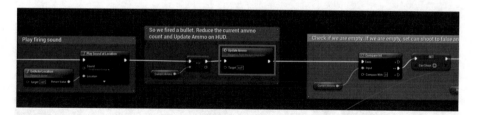

Figure 7-21. Calling Update Ammo after firing weapon

The third location is inside the Reload event. After setting the Can Shoot variable, call the Update Ammo function (see Figure 7-22).

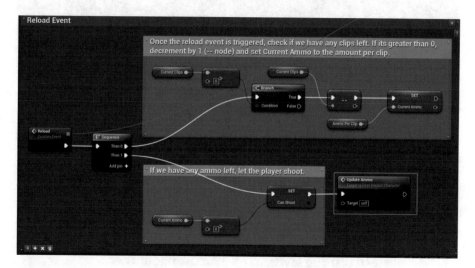

Figure 7-22. Calling Update Ammo after Reloading

If you press Play (Alt+P) now and shoot, you can see the ammo count updated correctly (see Figure 7-23).

Figure 7-23. *Ammo count updating on Player HUD*

Ammo Pickup

In Chapter 5, you learned how to create input keys and use tracing to
detect an item in front of us. As an exercise, I want you to recreate that
setup but with two differences.

1. Instead of using MyItemTrace for the name, use
   ItemPickup.

2. Set the start location of the trace to the world
   location of Sphere Component. Add this location to
   the multiply node and then connect the result to the
   Line Trace node's End input (see Figure 7-24).

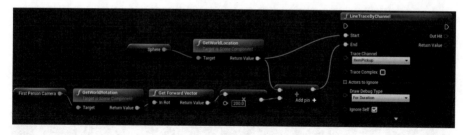

Figure 7-24. *Updating end location of Line Trace*

Right-click the graph, search for Input Action Trace, and select the Trace node. Connect the Trace node Pressed execution pin to the Line Trace By Channel node. You have the tracing setup done, for now, so let's create our Replenish ammo function, which grants us a single clip.

Create a new function and call it ReplenishAmmo. This function has no inputs, but you create a boolean output, which determines if the ammo was successfully replenished. To create an output, select the function (either in My Blueprint tab or open function graph and select the purple node), and in the Details panel, click the plus button under the Outputs category. This creates a new Return node with a boolean output.

Rename the NewParam output to bReturnValue. This function is responsible for adding a new clip under Max Clips. First, drag and drop the Current Clips variable into the graph (select Get CurrentClips in the context menu). Drag a wire from this variable, search for less, and select integer < integer node. CurrentClips is now automatically connected to the first input of < node. Let's drag and drop the MaxClips variable into the graph (select Get MaxClips in the context menu) and connect it to the second input of < node.

Create a Branch node and connect the output of < node to the Condition input of Branch input. If the current clips are less than max clips, the True output of the Branch node trigger drags a wire from Current Clips, search for Increment Int and select it. This is the same as Decrement Int except instead of subtracting by 1 this node add 1. Now drag and drop the Update Ammo function and connect it to the ++ node. After that,

155

connect this to the Return node and make sure the return value is true. Right-click the graph, search for Add Return node and select it. Connect this to the Branch node's False output and make sure it is set to False (see Figure 7-25).

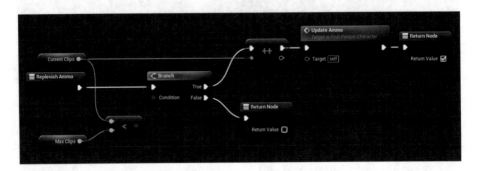

***Figure 7-25.** Replenish Ammo*

Go to Content Browser, create a new Blueprint class (Actor based), and call it BP_AmmoPickup. This is our class that grants the player a single ammo clip and destroys itself. Open our newly created actor (BP_AmmoPickup) and create a new custom event. Let's call it GiveAmmo and add a new input to this event, set the type to FirstPersonCharacter, and name it Character.

This input is our FirstPersonCharacter, so drag a wire from this input, search for Replenish Ammo and select it. Create a Branch node and connect the output of Replenish Ammo to this Branch node. Then right-click the graph, search for DestroyActor and select it. Connect the True output from the Branch node to the DestroyActor, and you are finished with this class (see Figure 7-26).

***Figure 7-26.** Give Ammo event*

Even though you have done our functions and events, you aren't using any of it yet, so let's fix that. Let's go back to the tracing setup. Create a new Branch node and connect the Return Value of Line Trace node to the Condition input of the Branch node. You only want to continue if the trace hits something.

Drag a wire from the Out Hit node and select Break Hit Result. Expand the Hit Result node by clicking the arrow button and drag a wire from the Hit actor pin. Search for Cast to BP_AmmoPickup node and select it. This is a handy node that tries to convert the given Object input to the respective type and triggers the first output if successful or Cast Failed if the conversion has failed.

Drag a wire from the output node labeled As BP Ammo Pickup and search for Give Ammo, which was the event you created. Select it, and you can see that it requires an input that should be the First Person Character class. Since you use the trace inside the First Person Character, right-click the graph and search for self and select Get a reference to self. The Self node outputs a reference to an instance of this Blueprint, so connect it to the Give Ammo input (see Figure 7-27).

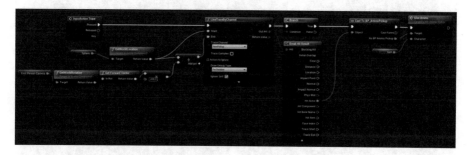

Figure 7-27. *Giving ammo from line trace result*

And you are done! Drag and drop the BP_AmmoPickup class into the game world and press Play (Alt+P). Keep shooting until you run out of ammo. And then go near an ammo pickup item in the world and press E to trace and pick up the item.

Package Game

The packaging game is a straightforward process. Packaging is the process of compiling and cooking the content in an optimized way for the target platform it is meant to run. When the packaging command is invoked, all the source code (if any) is compiled first. If the compilation is successful, then all the contents (Blueprints, Meshes, Textures, Materials, and so on) are converted (also known as cooking) into a special format that can be used by the target platform. Unreal Engine supports a wide variety of platforms, and from a Windows machine, you can compile and package for any platform except Apple Mac.

Each platform has its own settings that you can override. To do so, click Edit from the toolbar and select Project Settings (see Figure 7-28).

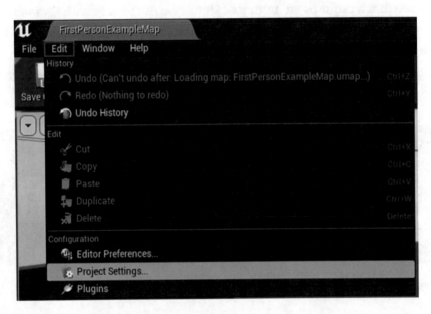

Figure 7-28. *Accessing project settings*

In Project Settings, on the right-side panel, scroll down until you reach the Platforms category. From this category, you can select your desired platform and override any settings (see Figure 7-29).

Figure 7-29. *Platform category*

To package your project, open Packaging Settings from File menu ➤
Package Project ➤ Packaging Settings (see Figure 7-30).

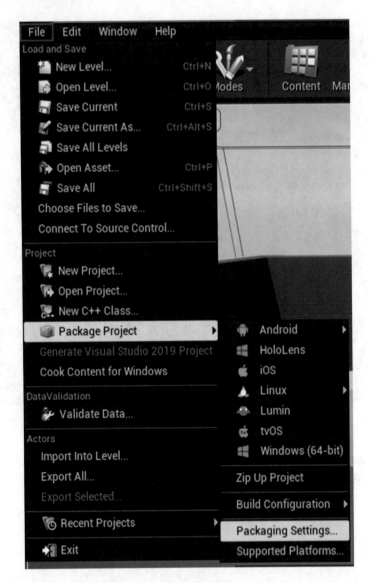

Figure 7-30. *Accessing packaging settings*

This opens the settings for packaging. In the settings window, under the Project category, switch the Build Configuration to Shipping and make sure the Full Rebuild and For Distribution checkboxes are turned on (see Figure 7-31).

Figure 7-31. *Selecting Shipping configuration*

Once you verify these settings, click File Menu again and select Windows (64-bit) from the Package Project menu. If this is the first time, Unreal Engine now prompts you to choose a location to save the packaged build. Navigate to your desired location and click Select Folder. Unreal Engine now starts packaging your build, and you see a toast notification on the button right corner of your screen (see Figure 7-32).

Figure 7-32. *Toast notification showing packaging for Windows*

You can click the Show Output Log on the Toast notification to see the build process.

Index

Printed in the United States
By Bookmasters